GROUP TECHNIQUES FOR IDEA BUILDING

Applied Social Research Methods Series
Volume 9

Applied Social Research Methods Series

Series Editor:
LEONARD BICKMAN, Peabody College, Vanderbilt University

Series Associate Editor:
DEBRA ROG, COSMOS Corporation, Washington, D.C.

This series is designed to provide students and practicing professionals in the social sciences with relatively inexpensive softcover textbooks describing the major methods used in applied social research. Each text introduces the reader to the state of the art of that particular method and follows step-by-step procedures in its explanation. Each author describes the theory underlying the method to help the student understand the reasons for undertaking certain tasks. Current research is used to support the author's approach. Examples of utilization in a variety of applied fields, as well as sample exercises, are included in the books to aid in classroom use.

Volumes in this series:

Additional volumes currently in development

GROUP TECHNIQUES FOR IDEA BUILDING

Carl M. Moore

Foreword by James Kunde

Applied Social Research Methods Series
Volume 9

SAGE PUBLICATIONS Newbury Park Beverly Hills London New Delhi

For information address:

SAGE Publications, Inc.
2111 West Hillcrest Drive
Newbury Park, California 91320

SAGE Publications Inc.
275 South Beverly Drive
Beverly Hills
California 90212

SAGE Publications Ltd.
28 Banner Street
London EC1Y 8QE
England

SAGE PUBLICATIONS India Pvt. Ltd.
M-32 Market
Greater Kailash I
New Delhi 110 048 India

Printed in the United States of America

Library of Congress Cataloging-in-Publication Data

Main entry under title:

Moore, Carl M.
  Group techniques.

  (Applied social research methods ; 9)
  Bibliography: p.
  1. Problem solving, Group. 2. Decision-making,
Group. 3. Social groups. I. Title. II. Series:
Applied social research methods series ; v. 9.
HM131.M615   1986   302.3   86-13731
ISBN 0-8039-2384-8
ISBN 0-8039-2385-6 (pbk.)

CONTENTS

FOREWORD
James Kunde

Carl Moore has undertaken a timely but difficult task. In the last decade, few themes have had more impact than the idea of using group processes to achieve results from various kinds of meetings. In the late 1960s, government administrators began to realize that hierarchical organizations weren't coping with the complexity of modern problems. I remember the confusion of a group of Dayton department heads in 1970 when—after a lengthy analysis of the current state of the city—it was concluded that the city organization was one of the most effective organizations it could be. But they also concluded that the city was "going to hell in a handbasket." That group jointly concluded that although the organization might be highly effective in delivering the services it was chartered to do, it was not having a significant effect on the complex forces that were causing negative changes in the community. The organizational changes that resulted extensively redesigned the system and developed task groups to come outside the bureaucracy and engage the community in an attack on comprehensive problems. That organization—and many others across the land—began dealing with "governance" as well as "service." Issues such as racism, housing, economic development, and neighborhood vitality became the equals of waste collection, airport maintenance, and dead animal removal.

But how could these governance issues be handled? It was clear that multiple disciplines and multiple interests were involved along with the knowledge and commitment of lay citizens. The traditional way of dealing with multiple interests was by committees. Committees had a bad reputation. Committees were often thought of as things that either functioned well if a strong chairman did all the work or didn't function at all—letting an issue atrophy through endless discussion. Clearly, a serious effort to attack complex problems needed something more effective than committees.

During the 1970s, the Kettering Foundation, among others, began research on how heterogeneous groups could work together more effectively. The Foundation's work in international relations—chiefly the Dartmouth Conference with U.S. and Soviet "Non-Governmental" Leaders—showed how carefully designed meetings could bring together vastly different interests and produce consensus. Followed up by action, the Foundation work in education concluded that the key to education reform was a school-level joint decision of the principal, teachers, and parents about how the school should be improved. The Foundation's later work on urban policy issues applied the lessons of the other programs. Groups using effective meeting designs were capable of producing ideas and commitments that could solve problems that even the best hierarchical organizations couldn't begin to deal with.

Carl Moore has been a pioneer of the group process movement. He, along with his late cohort Jim Coke, designed and implemented processes for helping groups of elected officials to deal with policy tasks more effectively. They introduced computer-assisted meeting techniques that enormously simplified the ability of elected and appointed officers to deal with complex interrelationships but were simple enough to be easily understood and trusted. They designed processes for large major meetings—including three White House conferences—that enabled those sessions to wade through enormous complexity and produce useful policy recommendations.

The idea of group process to make meetings successful is an idea now well accepted by some busy government, business, and nonprofit executives. However, although the idea has become accepted by some, it has been the province of a relatively small number of skilled facilitators. Carl Moore delivers here a clear explanation of the basic processes most useful to facilitators in a variety of circumstances. He illustrates how they can be applied by the people who normally manage meetings: citizens, administrators, and business executives. Carl's advice is a straightforward and practical summary of a decade of experimentation and proven results.

American governance has always relied on the ability of average citizens, both inside and outside of government, to come together and agree on actions needed to solve problems. The complexity of today's world requires that the "coming together" be analytical, efficient, and creative.

During the past two decades, America has spent great energy empowering groups that have been denied a place at this coming together. The overwhelming question today is this: How can all the empowered now deal creatively with problems that are often international in scope and multidisciplinary in character? Effective group processes aren't all of the answer, but they can be the most critical first step.

PREFACE

The goal of this book is to explicate four techniques that can be utilized by groups of people to manage complexity; that is, to generate, develop, and select between ideas. Chapter 1 will briefly introduce the techniques and provide a rationale for focusing on them.

My justification for including a book on group techniques (in general, and these techniques in particular) in a series on applied social research is that whenever the conceptual work of research is about the functioning of groups, is conducted by a group, or uses groups, the techniques described in this book should be useful.

All four techniques can be utilized in order *to answer research questions.* For example, if you wanted to know the principal needs of the elderly in Kent, Ohio, you might choose to use one or more of the techniques to answer that question. Chapter 4 provides an illustration of how Nominal Group Technique and Delphi Technique were used together to answer a similar question for the elderly citizens of a Michigan community.

Similarly, you could use the techniques to involve groups in answering questions such as

- What do members of the legal profession perceive to be the issues that should be addressed by social science researchers?
- Which work activities have priority for the county commissioners?
- How can learning disabilities be characterized so that children can be grouped for instruction?

The descriptions of each technique provided in the following chapters include examples of how the techniques were used to answer applied research questions.

A common research application is to use the techniques *to facilitate the conduct of research.* Each of the techniques can be used during the *design* of a research project to clarify the focus of the project and to ensure that the design is on track with the research client's expectations. They can be used during the *implementation* of a research project to collect opinions and attitudes and to achieve consensus on topics or issues. They can be used in the *final stage* of a research project to generate recommendations for action based on the research results and to establish priorities among the findings that need attention. A group technique may also serve as a *research validation tool*, to corroborate and amplify data collected through a more quantitative technique. The techniques can be used whenever it is desirable to collaborate in conducting research.

Researchers might choose *to conduct research about the techniques.* For example, you might have an idea about how to modify one of the techniques and want to have empirical verification of whether the modification achieves the purpose for which it was designed. Research could be conducted in order to test the *purposes* for which the techniques have been designed and used. Does the Delphi Technique, for example, produce more accurate short-term predictions than some other technique? Is it effective in reducing the undesirable impact on group participation by persons who have higher status or additional power within the group? Research could also be conducted on the *implementation* of the steps or stages of individual techniques. For example, it may be possible to study what is the largest number of items a group of policymakers can be expected to consider during the course of an Interpretive Structural Modeling (ISM) session. Also, research could be conducted on the *relationships between the techniques*, such as whether Nominal Group Technique or Ideawriting should be used to develop the items to be presented on the first round of a Policy Delphi (which is differentiated from a traditional Delphi because it begins with a set of ideas gleaned from a source—group of people, literature review, etc.—other than the participants in the Delphi).

Chapter 1 will briefly discuss a rationale for using a group, rather than a single individual, to conduct research.

ACKNOWLEDGMENTS

In preparing this book I have been more collator than author. My debt to certain people and a few institutions is great. James Guthrie Coke allowed me to tag along as he solved problems. Together we came to realize the power in using techniques that would enable a wide variety of groups to be productive and to feel good about themselves. Many of the examples I relate were projects we did together. Jim and I coauthored the original versions of the materials on Nominal Group Technique and Ideawriting.

An earlier version of the materials on Nominal Group Technique and Ideawriting were prepared for and published by the Academy for Contemporary Problems, a wonderful environment within which to work. It certainly was nice to have a chance to experiment in using techniques to address meaningful societal problems. People like Ralph Widner and Ken Rainey were intellectual entrepreneurs in the best sense of that word.

Another place that continues to give me an opportunity to address important problems is the Kettering Foundation. The Kettering Foundation encouraged me to "try things" because they thought the old approaches could be improved upon, and, most importantly, they have worked with me so I learned more about the doing. Life will not be as much fun if my name doesn't come to Jim Kunde's or Chris Carlson's minds when someone asks them how to deal with a complex contemporary problem. Jim authored Chapter 9 on the role of a process observer.

A sabbatical from Kent State University enabled me to split a year between the Kettering Foundation and what was then called the Center for Interactive Management, School of Engineering and Applied Sciences, University of Virginia. Every sabbatical ought to be as restful, as exhilarating, and as productive as was mine. The highpoint was the opportunity to work almost daily with John Warfield. John invented two of the techniques I describe in the book—Ideawriting and Interpretive Structural Modeling. He is passionately committed to making this world a better place by improving how groups work together in order to solve problems. John gathered at the center some interesting, productive, and nice people, such as Bill Woods, Aleco Christakis, and David Keener. It was during my stay at the Center that I had an opportunity to finish the description of Interpretive Structural Modeling and draft two of the application chapters. F. Ross Janes, who contributes Chapter 8, was my colleague at the Center. He was there on a sabbatical from the Department of Systems Engineering, City University, London.

An original version of the description of ISM was prepared with Jack Gargan, my colleague at Kent State, and Ken Parker, at the time a graduate student at Kent State. Ken's work on this project was part of his responsibility as the James Coke Fellow in Public Management, sponsored by the Academy for Contemporary Problems.

Allen Bukoff was responsible for preparing for publication most of the figures that appear in the book, which is fitting since we have worked together for years, and he was responsible for the original design of many of them. Whenever I do a project with Allen it is always better than if I had done the work alone or with someone who does not have his talent or integrity.

My greatest debt is to Linda, Chris, and Lee because they have loved me enough to allow me to spend considerable time away from home using the techniques and processes of this book to help groups to generate, develop, and select ideas.

—Carl M. Moore
Kent State University

1

Techniques of Choice

This chapter introduces four task-oriented group techniques that are the "techniques of choice" when assisting groups in conducting applied social research. The chapter includes sections on why groups should be used in conducting applied social research, why the book focuses on these particular techniques, and what have been principal influences on the development and use of the four techniques.

This book provides clear, useful descriptions of four task-oriented group techniques: Nominal Group Technique (NGT), Ideawriting, Delphi Technique, and Interpretive Structural Modeling (ISM).

Nominal Group Technique is a method for structuring small group meetings that allows individual judgments to be effectively pooled and used in situations in which uncertainty or disagreement exists about the nature of a problem or possible solutions. NGT typically includes four steps: silent generation of ideas in writing, round-robin recording of ideas, serial discussion of the listed ideas, and voting to determine the most important ideas.

Ideawriting, a group method for developing ideas and exploring their meaning, is particularly helpful in making more specific the general ideas that result from group interactions and in generating ideas. Ideawriting focuses on a single topic, requires a relatively brief time, and produces a written product. It typically includes four steps: organization (of a large group into small groups), initial response (in writing), written interaction, and analysis and reporting of the written interaction.

The *Delphi Technique* was named after the Oracle at Delphi, Greece, because it was first used to forecast future events. Delphi utilizes a series of mail questionnaires to aggregate the knowledge, judgments, or opinions of anonymous experts in order to address complex questions.

Interpretive Structural Modeling is a method for identifying and summarizing relationships among specific items that define an issue or problem. ISM provides a means by which a group can impose order on the complexity of those items. The method is "interpretive" in that the group's judgment decides whether and how items are related. It is "structural" in that an overall structure is extracted from the complex set of items on the basis of the relationships. And it is "modeling" in that the specific relationships and overall structure are portrayed in graphic form.

All four techniques are formulary responses to the group constraints of time, space, and people. Specific steps are followed in each technique in order to overcome the problems that typically plague interacting groups. Therefore, the techniques are presented didactically with emphasis on the *stages* of the techniques. For each technique, stages or steps are identified that should be closely followed if the technique is to be used effectively.

The techniques normally are used to enable small groups of people to address a specific planning or decision-making task and are often used in combination.

The next four chapters describe the techniques: Nominal Group Technique is presented in Chapter 2, Ideawriting in Chapter 3, the Delphi Technique in Chapter 4, and Interpretive Structural Modeling in Chapter 5. Chapters 6, 7, 8, and 9 also focus on Interpretive Structural Modeling. As ISM is conceptually and technically more complex than the other three techniques, attention is given to a variety of issues: how to review an ISM product, how to cope with a large number of elements in an ISM, how *not* to phrase a subordination relation, and the role of a process observer in an ISM session. Chapter 10 describes how the techniques are linked together in order to enable groups to achieve their goals. Chapter 11 provides criteria that can be used to guide your decision regarding when to use each of the techniques, and Chapter 12, called "Beyond Techniques," summarizes some principles that are useful for a group leader to keep in mind whether or not he or she is using a particular technique.

The examples used to illustrate the techniques are drawn from my experiences helping public groups, such as elected officials, government agencies, and neighborhood citizen organizations, plan for the future. Use of the techniques, however, is not limited to public decision making. They can be used by any kind of group to improve productivity and, as indicated by this volume's inclusion in a series on applied research methods, each of the techniques can be especially useful in conducting applied social research.

WHY USE GROUPS IN CONDUCTING
APPLIED SOCIAL RESEARCH?

The question that heads this section—Why use groups in conducting applied social research?—can be asked another way: Why use groups to address social problems? The answer is in the question: "Social" problems exist because society chooses to function in groups. As the group has the problem, they have to discover the solution that will work for them.

Another meaning to the question is this: Why use a group of people, rather than an individual, in conducting research? There are at least four important reasons it is desirable to use groups when conducting applied social research. *A group can do some things better than an individual.* When it was pointed out to Olaf Helmer, the inventor of the Delphi Technique, that there is "no conclusive theoretical explanation why or how the Delphi Technique does what it does," his response was that "it is logical that if you properly combine the judgment of a large number of people, you have a better chance of getting closer to the truth" (Helmer, 1981, p. 83). If you want to identify items for a test, develop an instrument, think through the implications of a research design, or discover the attitudes of a segment of the population, you are likely to do better if you use a group. After all, two or more heads are usually better than one: *pooled intelligence.*

The second reason it is desirable to use groups in conducting applied social research is that *in order to understand social phenomena, it often is necessary to obtain the views of the actors.* Certain group techniques, such as those presented in this book, enable the researcher to obtain the views of the critical actors. It is usually more desirable to ask citizens in a community what their needs are rather than depend upon a review of the literature to tell you what they are likely to be. A literature review probably is going to provide you with generalizations that do not necessarily reflect a particular reality.

The third reason is that *it is often beneficial to use groups if you are concerned about the consequences of your research.* If your goal is to solve a problem of a particular group, it is reasonable to believe that the group is more likely to accept your advice (or research findings) if they have participated in the research process. This becomes a special issue when you are conducting applied social research that has political implications. (And virtually all important problems are likely to have substantial political consequences!) If you want to effect policy, it is wise to include those responsible for acting on the policy. Research on knowledge and research utilization has found that a critical factor in the usefulness and use of research is decision-maker involvement in the research process, which can only occur if there is communication between decision makers and researchers (e.g., Weiss, 1977). The group setting is the context for such communication.

The fourth reason is that *complex, ill-defined problems often can be addressed only by pooled intelligence.* Virtually all societal problems, which are the problems likely to be addressed by applied researchers, are complex, value-laden, and ill-defined (Olsen, 1982, p. 65; Strauch, 1974). Because societal problems are value-laden, it is often appropriate to use groups to conduct applied social research. As explained earlier, this is especially true when it is necessary to involve the actors, either to obtain their knowledge and opinions or to assure the acceptance of the research effort. Groups may be used in conjunction with other research methods (e.g., a group could be used to help develop a questionnaire that would then be administered by a single researcher, or even a team, using traditional methods for conducting survey research) or may be the only approach taken by the applied researcher.

Quantitative research methods—which identify and attempt to study variables of human behavior, usually in a controlled setting—often are not suitable to address complex, ill-defined problems. Figure 1.1 posits that quantification is most useful when a problem is well-defined. The assumption is that the clearer the variable is, the more it lends itself to measurement/quantification. Quantification can be and often is a central feature of research that addresses well-defined problems. As problems become increasingly complex, and therefore ill-defined, quantification becomes less useful. Consequently, measurement/quantification is likely to be emphasized less and to be more peripheral when the research problem is ill-defined.

In sum, the reasons that groups should be used in conducting applied social research are as follows: A group can do some things better than an individual; it is often necessary to obtain the views of the actors—those who have the problem that needs to be addressed; the outcomes of the research are more likely to be accepted if you involve those who

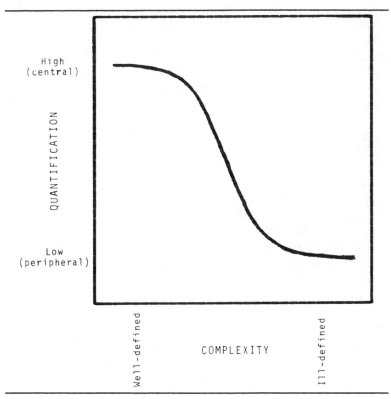

Figure 1.1   Relationship of Complexity and Quantification

have to act on the problem; and complex, ill-defined problems often can be addressed only by groups.

WHY THESE FOUR TECHNIQUES?

I have chosen to focus on these four particular techniques because my experience reveals that they are the preferred ways to help groups of people to manage ideas (i.e., to assist them in generating, developing, or selecting between ideas). They are clearly superior to other options. For example, Nominal Group Technique is likely to produce a better product and a higher degree of group satisfaction than other ways of generating ideas, such as Brainstorming. Ideawriting takes less time to address a topic than an interacting group and produces a written product that can be saved. Delphi enables one to use a group that cannot or should not come together. Moreover, it allows the group to realize a collective perspective with a minimum of group frustration. Interpretive Structural Modeling enables a group to produce a dynamic outcome that is likely to be more useful to the group than typical ways of selecting between ideas, such as parliamentary procedure and voting.

All of the techniques meet the rationale for using groups in conducting applied social research. They provide a way

- for a group of people to produce a product that is superior to what they could produce individually,
- to obtain the views of the actors (in that they enable you to use the time of the participants efficiently and productively, so that people are willing to participate),
- to create a commitment on the part of the participants for the product that is produced, and
- for groups to address complex, ill-defined societal problems.

The next section, which presents the principal "influences" on the development and use of these four techniques, suggests additional reasons why these are preferred ways to work with groups. They help to overcome the problems that occur in traditional interacting groups, they allow the people who are likely to be effected by the change to plan for change, they enable groups to focus on specific tasks and to be dependent upon themselves rather than on experts for solving their problems, and they provide ways to generate, develop, and select between ideas.

PRINCIPAL INFLUENCES ON THE DEVELOPMENT
AND USE OF THESE TECHNIQUES

The study of group behavior is a relatively recent intellectual pursuit, confined essentially to the twentieth century. The techniques described in this book have become popularized during the last ten years. Although the Delphi Technique was invented in the early 1950s, the first substantial explication of its various forms, along with a variety of applications, was published in the mid-1970s (Linstone & Turoff,

1975). The first extensive criticism of the technique was published about the same time (Sackman, 1975). Nominal Group Technique and Ideawriting are based on work in creativity, particularly on Osborne's work with brainstorming begun in the 1930s, but were introduced in print in 1975 by Delbecq and associates and in 1976 by Warfield. Interpretive Structural Modeling, founded on various branches of mathematics, was introduced in book form in the middle 1970s (Warfield, 1976).

There are a number of convergent influences that help to explain the creation of and interest in using the techniques. These "influences" are overlapping and interrelated; they are separated only so that they can be identified and described.

All four of the techniques were created in order to overcome problems that typically occur in groups. Nominal Group Technique was specifically designed to circumvent factors that have an adverse impact on groups, such as verbal aggressiveness and status; to enable groups to generate more alternatives than the limited number they would produce in a traditional interacting group; and to allow a group to be effective even if the members of the group do not know one another (Delbecq, Van de Ven, & Gustafson, 1975). Delphi keeps individuals separated and anonymous in order to reduce the influence of blocs of people or the personalities of certain individuals; to allow strangers to communicate effectively; to allow for the participation of more people than could be effective in an interacting group; and to prevent unproductive disagreements (Linstone & Turoff, 1975). Ideawriting controls the inhibiting influence on groups of verbal aggressiveness; provides people with the opportunity to clearly phrase their thoughts before speaking; and allows groups to have a permanent, rather than an ephemeral, record of their deliberations (Warfield, 1976). Interpretive Structural Modeling has as one of its goals to improve the quality of public debate by enabling a group to manage the complexity of ideas they have to consider (Warfield, 1976).

I asked a group of expert group facilitators, all of whom had experience working with the techniques presented in this book, why techniques such as NGT, Ideawriting, Delphi, and ISM should be utilized in order to conduct applied social research. They contended that the use of such techniques can improve the quality of virtually any kind of meeting (but particularly meetings between people who do not have a history of working together) by improving the group's productivity, eliminating confusion, promoting appreciation of the realities that need to be considered by the group, inventing alternatives, using time wisely, and circumventing many of the problems inherent in group activity. The problems they identified that these techniques eliminate or reduce include when a group produces only a *few ideas,* when a group is *dominated* by one (or a few) of its members, when there is a lack of *participation* by all of the group members, when a group distorts its product because members respond too strongly to the *status* of one (or a few) of the group members, or when the group is unduly influenced by *political problems* (such as the authority of an elected chairperson or the established rules of procedure used to conduct meetings).

A basic tenet in applying the techniques has been adopted from *organizational development*: Planning for organizational change should involve those who are likely to be affected by the change. The techniques presented in this book facilitate the participation of a wide range of people by (1) helping reduce the influence that people of status have on the group's productivity (Who can be honest with the boss in the room?); (2) enabling a substantial amount of work to be accomplished in a brief time period (I cannot take the time away from my job for nonessential activities like planning!); (3) facilitating contact with people who are separated by distance and who cannot come together conveniently; and (4) enabling people who do not have a history of working together to work effectively in groups.

During the 1960s and early 1970s a great deal of emphasis was placed on the *socioemotional development of groups.* Sensitivity training was big business. A variety of approaches to helping individuals and groups came to be called the Human Potential Movement. As a reaction against this movement and what its critics called the "touchy feely" approach to groups, emphasis was placed on the development of techniques that could help groups to become productive by accomplishing *tasks.* Thus, interest in the techniques described in this book has been due at least in part to a reaction against what was perceived as the exclusive and excessive focus on group "health." Helping a group to accomplish its task often has the consequence of improving members' interpersonal relations and, consequently, the group's "health."

Professional problem solving traditionally has been predicated on the belief that select, well-trained individuals (experts!) could analyze a problem and then apply their tools to solving the problem, virtually independent of those who had the problem. This view of professional problem solving was characterized by a set of assumptions, such as these:

- There is professional expertise that can be applied to other people's problems.
- The design process is a process wherein the professional [becomes informed] about a client's problems and then formulates a solution on the basis of...professional expertise.
- Any "publicizing" or exposure of the means by which decisions are reached is unnecessary because [a] professional is guided by [a] code of ethics.
- The development of increasingly complex techniques and procedures leads to better solutions, albeit at the cost of making the professional designer increasingly indispensable. (Olsen, 1982, p. 7)

In the early 1970s, a different set of assumptions, called *second-generation design methods*, emerged. Some of the assumptions are as follows:

- Expertise does not reside solely in the professional, but in all those whose interests are affected by a design or planning problem.
- Planning and design should be viewed as an argumentative process or as a network of issues to be argued and decided.
- Any given issue can always be viewed as a symptom of some more fundamental one.
- A client who delegates judgment to a professional must be able to maintain control over the delegated judgment.
- The designer/planner conspires with his client to develop a solution, thus eliminating the problem of getting one's proposals implemented by his participation in producing the proposal. (Olsen, 1982, p. 9)

There are other important points of comparison between first- and second-generation design methods.

First-Generation Methods	*Second-Generation Methods*
Process	
linear, sequential phasing of design activities	iterative activities carried out simultaneously
View of the Solution	
solution is fairly well defined at the outset	no clear-cut image of the solution
Methods	
scientific, systematic, quantitative, objective	systems, "political," participatory, holistic

	Participants
experts, specialists	participation by heterogeneous group of people (all with a stake or interest in the outcome)

The four techniques presented in this book fall primarily within the assumptions of second-generation design methods because they typically are used to address ill-defined problems that require the participation of those who are (or will be) responsible for the problem and solution. An individual or group who is responsible for the solution is not likely to completely relinquish control over the process. Such a group is likely to be heterogeneous, particularly in terms of status—involving policymakers as well as those who have a direct stake in the outcome. Because the problem is "ill-defined," there is no clear-cut image of the solution.

Experts cannot solve such problems; they do not know enough (Lindblom & Cohen, 1979), their analyses are opaque (often even to themselves); that is, the direction of their findings is seldom unequivocal, their communication to policymakers—who must act on the knowledge that they have been provided—is seldom clear, and they are not accountable to any constituency for mistakes (Warfield, 1982).

John Warfield, when he was director of the Center for Interactive Management within the School of Engineering and Applied Science at the University of Virginia, explained that the set of methodologies the Center used to address a given problem of management or planning must include at least one methodology that identifies problems, goals, and norms (*intelligence*); at least one that conceptualizes alternatives (*design*); and at least one that allows for the selection of the preferred alternative (*choice*). The four techniques presented in this book meet his criteria. Nominal Group Technique is essentially a way to *generate* ideas (intelligence); Ideawriting and Delphi can be used to generate ideas but are primarily ways to *develop* ideas (design); and Interpretive Structural Modeling is a way to *select* ideas (choice).

SUMMARY

It is desirable to use groups in conducting applied social research because a group can do some things better than an individual, it is often necessary to obtain the views of the actors (those who have the problem that needs to be addressed), the outcome of the research is more likely to be accepted if you involve those who have to act on the problem, and complex, ill-defined problems often can be addressed only by working with a group that can provide pooled intelligence.

This book describes four task-oriented group techniques—Nominal Group Technique, Ideawriting, Delphi Technique, and Interpretive Structural Modeling—that are preferred ways to assist groups in conducting applied social research.

Some of the principal influences on the development and use of these techniques have been the desire to improve the operations of inter-acting groups, the assumption of organizational development that people should participate in solving their own problems, the emergence of second-generation design methods, the development of techniques to help groups accomplish tasks, and the need to use groups in order to manage the complexity of ideas by providing intelligence, design, and choice.

2

Nominal Group Technique

This chapter describes Nominal Group Technique and includes sections on premeeting preparations, the opening statement, conducting the NGT process, and using NGT in a large group. An extended example of the technique, along with sections on limitations and resources, are also included.

Nominal Group Technique (NGT) is a method for structuring small group meetings that allows individual judgments to be effectively pooled and used in situations in which uncertainty or disagreement exists about the nature of a problem and possible solutions. The process has been used extensively in business and government and has proven especially beneficial in fostering citizen participation in program planning.

The technique is helpful in identifying problems, exploring solutions, and establishing priorities. It works particularly well in "stranger groups," in which it is important to neutralize differences in status and verbal dominance among group members.

NGT typically includes four steps:

(1) *Silent generation of ideas in writing*: Working silently and independently, participants jot down their responses to a stimulus question.
(2) *Round-robin recording of ideas*: When called upon, each participant contributes a single idea that is recorded on a large flip-chart. Discussion of the ideas is not permitted. Completed sheets are taped to the wall so that they can be seen by the group. The group facilitator continues to call upon the participants until all ideas have been recorded or the group determines that they have produced a sufficient number of ideas.
(3) *Serial discussion of the list of ideas*: The participants discuss each idea on the list so that they are clear about the meaning of the ideas.
(4) *Voting*: The participants identify what each of them believes are the most important ideas, they rank-order their preferences, the votes are recorded on the flip-chart, and the voting pattern is discussed.

Based on my experience, the ideal size of an NGT group is 5 to 9 members. Larger groups can be handled by making minor changes in procedure, particularly in Step 2 (see below), but any group larger than 12 or 13 should be divided.

With an average-size group, the entire process can be comfortably completed in 90 minutes. By limiting Steps 2 and 3, it is possible for a group to go through the process in just over an hour. In no case should the session be permitted to last over three hours.

There are three NGT essentials: (1) a carefully prepared question that evokes responses at the desired level of specificity; (2) a group of task-oriented individuals with expertise in the topic (do not be put off by the word "expertise"; citizens are expert on their needs, college students know most about their tastes); and (3) a group leader who has mastered the process and is willing to act as a process facilitator, not a substantive expert.

PREMEETING PREPARATIONS

There are four essential preparations that have to be made before the meeting by the group facilitator:

(1) Formulate and test the NGT question: The facilitator should pay careful attention to the phrasing of the question. It should be as *simple* as possible, but it should *elicit items at the desired level of specificity and abstraction*. NGT is a *single-question* technique. A poor NGT question would be, "What are the goals to be achieved and the projects and programs to be undertaken by the city's community development program?" The question is poor because it is complex and, consequently, it will be difficult to analyze the ideas produced. A good NGT question would be, "What obstacles do you anticipate to carrying out the city's housing rehabilitation programs?"

Several people should be involved in preparing the question. They should begin by clarifying the objectives of the meeting. They should then illustrate the types of items they want to get from the group. With objectives and examples in mind, they can proceed to the composition of the question.

The NGT question should be *pilot tested*, if there is time, to make sure that it evokes the desired type of response. A propitious time for such testing is when prospective group leaders are being trained to conduct NGT sessions.

(2) Assemble supplies, including a flip-chart (or easel with newsprint or large sheets of paper—butcher-type paper or newspaper end-rolls that can be taped to the wall), water-based (rather than permanent) felt-tip pens that will not bleed through the paper, masking tape, and 3×5 cards for each group. The NGT question should be typed at the top of a sheet of paper and duplicated for each member.

(3) Prepare the meeting room: Wall surfaces should be suitable for taping up sheets from the flip-chart. The best table arrangement is an open "U," with the flip-chart located at the open end.

(4) Train inexperienced group leaders: If the group leaders have never conducted an NGT session, you should arrange a training session that simulates the process. For training purposes, good NGT questions are either the actual (or potential) question the group is planning to use or the general question, "What barriers do you anticipate in using NGT in your own organization (or agency or committee)?" If the actual question is used, the training session is an occasion to pilot test the phrasing of the NGT question.

OPENING STATEMENT

The opening statement is important because it can set the tone for the whole meeting. It should include at least three elements:

(1) The importance of the task and the unique contributions of each group member should be noted.
(2) The group should be informed of the session's overall goal and how the NGT results will be used.
(3) The four basic steps of NGT should be briefly summarized.

When a large group is to be divided, it is best to present the opening statement at a plenary session before each NGT group begins its work. That way everyone will be operating under the same set of procedures.

CONDUCTING THE NGT PROCESS

Step 1: Silent Generation of Ideas in Writing

Distribute the question on individual sheets of paper or display it before the group. Read the question aloud to the group and ask members to respond to it by writing their ideas in phrases or brief sentences. Remind them that, because you will not be collecting their lists, good penmanship is unimportant.

Ask members to work silently and independently. Demonstrate good behavior by doing your own silent writing. Immediately stop disruptive behavior, such as talking.

Some members may ask about the meaning of the NGT question. You may illustrate the degree of abstraction desired or call upon one of the members of the group to do so, but do not lead the group in any direction. Tell persistent questioners to respond to the NGT question in whatever way is most meaningful to them.

Allow four to eight minutes for this step. In a large group, a short period of silent writing will appropriately limit the number of items the members produce.

Step 2: Round-Robin Recording of Ideas

Explain that the objective of this step is to map the group's thinking. As you go around the table, each member is to present orally one idea from his or her own list in a phrase or brief sentence without discussion, elaboration, or justification. You will continue to go around the table until all ideas have been presented.

Explain that each member is to decide whether his or her item duplicates one already presented. A member may pass at any time, but may reenter the process later in his or her turn. Continue to call on members who have passed. Encourage members to "hitchhike" on others' ideas and to add new items, even though these items may not have been written down during Step 1.

The leader should record items on flip-chart sheets as rapidly as possible, numbering items in sequence and recording them in the members' own words. If possible, avoid condensing and abbreviating. It is very important that the participants know that they have produced the items and that the list belongs to them, not you. Ask long-winded participants to come up with simpler wording. If this causes delay, tell the person you will return for a shorter phrase and move on to the next member.

After you fill a sheet with numbered items, tape it to the wall where it will be visible to everyone. If you have someone to assist you, he or she can tape up the sheets while you continue with the round-robin recording. Another option that can expedite the process is to ask one of the group members to assist you by taping sheets to the wall.

With a large group, the length of the list can be controlled in several ways. For example, you can announce in advance that you will solicit items around the table only two or three times. Or, when a sufficient number of items have been generated, say that you will go around the table only once more and they should give you the best item remaining on their sheets.

Step 3: Serial Discussion of the Listed Ideas

Explain that the purpose of this step is to clarify the ideas presented. Read each item aloud in sequence and invite comments. Members may note their agreement or disagreement, but arguments are unnecessary as each person will vote independently in Step 4. Do not waste time on conflict. As soon as the logic of a position is clear, cut off discussion. The meaning of most items will be obvious to the group and little or no discussion will be necessary.

Announce in advance the number of minutes to be devoted to this step. The usual rule of thumb is to allot two minutes times the number of items. If time is short, allow only the number of minutes until adjournment, minus fifteen minutes for the voting in Step 4.

Encourage viewing the list as group property. Anyone can clarify or comment on any item. If someone asks about the meaning of one of the items, it is productive to encourage someone other than the contributor of the particular item to clarify what it means to him or her. The group leader can model good behavior at an appropriate point with a comment such as, "Well, to me this item means. ..."

Within reason, new items can be added and small editorial changes made. Duplicate items may also be combined. However, the leader should resist attempts to combine many items into broader categories. Some members may seek to achieve consensus by this means, and the precision of the original items may be lost.

Step 4: Voting

Ranking is the simplest and usually most effective voting technique. Sometimes ratings are used, with each of the seven most important items on a list rated on a one-to-seven-scale. Ranking is usually preferable, however, because it can be quickly tallied and the results are easily interpreted.

Each person should receive five 3 × 5 cards (seven cards if the list is long). Ask members to select the five most important items and write one in the center of each card. They should write the item's sequence number in the upper left corner. Tell them not to be concerned with

```
┌─────────────────────────────────────────────────────────┐
│  6                                                        │
│                                                           │
│               PARKING SPACES RESERVED                     │
│                                                           │
│               FOR HANDICAPPED                             │
│                                                           │
│                                                           │
└─────────────────────────────────────────────────────────┘
```

penmanship; the only purpose for writing the item on the card is so that they will not have to refer back to the sheets on the wall when they rank-order their five cards.

Give the group a time limit (four or five minutes) for selecting its priority items and do a countdown (e.g., "You have two minutes left"). Request that the group members work silently, and that they wait until everyone is finished before rank-ordering the cards. Everyone will rank-order their choices together.

When everyone has completed the set of five cards, announce that the rank-ordering will begin. Go through the following instructions without delay, using this general wording.

Spread the cards out in front of you so that you can see all five at once. Decide which card is more important than all the others. Write "5" in the lower right-hand corner and underline it three times. Turn the card over.

```
┌─────────────────────────────────────────────────────────┐
│  6                                                        │
│                                                           │
│               PARKING SPACES RESERVED                     │
│                                                           │
│               FOR HANDICAPPED                             │
│                                                           │
│                                              5            │
│                                              ═            │
└─────────────────────────────────────────────────────────┘
```

Which is the least important of the four remaining cards? Write "1" in the lower right corner and underline it three times. Turn the card over.

Select the most important of the three remaining cards. Write "4" in the lower right corner and underline it three times. Turn the card over.

Select the least important of the two cards that are left. Write "2" in the lower right corner and underline it three times.

Write "3" in the lower right corner of the last card and underline it three times.

Collect the cards (I shuffle them together to communicate to the participants that no one is going to pay attention to how each person voted), and record the vote on the flip-chart in front of the group. You can prepare a tally sheet while the group is making their voting decisions.

VOTE

1.	13.
2.	14.
3.	15.
4.	16.
5.	17.
6.	18.
7.	19.
8.	20.
9.	21.
10.	22.
11.	23.
12.	24.

If someone is assisting you, ask them (or one of the members of the group) to read off the votes to you: "Item number 13 got a 3." The reason for having them underline their ranking three times is so that you can tell the difference between the number of the item and how they ranked the item. Tally rankings alongside the columns of item numbers. The example below shows how a group of six members voted on a list of 24 items.

VOTE

1. 2,1,1,1	13. 3,3
2.	14. 4
3. 5,4,5,5,3,4	15.
4. 3,2	16.
5. 5	17. 4,3,3,1
6.	18. 2
7. 5	19. 1
8.	20.

9. 2	21. 4
10. 1	22.
11. 2	23.
12. 5,4,2	24.

Lead a discussion of the voting pattern. The number of votes an item gets is likely to be the most important indication of its relative priority. Resist the temptation to play numerical games, such as adding the rankings together to arrive at a consolidated score. In the above example, adding the scores would obscure the different patterns of support for items 1 and 5: that four different members of the group thought that item 1 was one of their most important items.

If time permits, the group can further clarify the items and vote again. Keep the discussion brief, and caution people not to change their minds frivolously.

USING NGT IN A LARGE GROUP

With a large group, begin with a plenary session at which you present the opening statement. Then divide the group into subgroups of five to nine persons and conduct simultaneous NGT sessions. Separate meeting rooms are preferable, but it is possible to use one large room if the acoustics and wall space are suitable.

Often a large group meeting will be finished as soon as the individual NGT groups have produced their product. The groups may come together for a plenary session at which each of the small groups report their results and a monitoring group will then be responsible for analyzing the products that have been generated. Occasionally the group will want to consolidate the separate products and produce one single, prioritized list that represents the work of the full group.

Consolidating Lists

It may be desirable to consolidate the lists of each subgroup. Allow at least 90 minutes (two hours is better) for the group facilitators to meet and create a master list. The participants should be occupied elsewhere with a plenary session of some type, such as a luncheon or a panel discussion.

An efficient procedure for consolidating lists is to begin with each group facilitator describing the items that received the strongest support in the group's voting. Through discussion, the facilitators will agree on two types of strongly supported items: (1) duplicate items that should be reworded and (2) items unique to a single group. The latter can be transferred with only minor editing to the master list. The former require much more care in rewording because you are trying to reflect the meanings of different groups with one statement.

Plenary Session Voting

The master list is likely to have between 15 and 25 items, a manageable size for discussion. It should be written on flip-chart sheets and placed on the wall of the meeting room.

The group then reassembles in plenary session. A facilitator leads a serial discussion of the master list in order to clarify the meaning of each item and to add items if desired. The group should be given a number of opportunities to add items that they believe were important in their small group session but that have been left off of the consolidated list. Otherwise, the participants will become suspicious that an attempt has been made to manipulate the list. The group then votes as in Step 4. The vote is tabulated and displayed before the group.

AN EXAMPLE

The political leaders of a rural region, composed of three counties that encompass an Indian tribe and numerous governmental entities, was preparing to negotiate with the state and federal governments. Their goal was to improve the region by obtaining legislative and financial concessions. Before a credible proposal could go forward, it was necessary for the leaders of the area to be able to describe what the citizens desired.

The decision was made to hold a communitywide meeting to ascertain the desires of the citizens. First, it was necessary to have a planning meeting in order to build the agenda for the community meeting and to identify who should be invited to the meeting. Nominal Group Technique was used in order to accomplish the latter task.

Seven people and a facilitator sat around an oval-shaped table in a small conference room. All of the persons had been asked to attend the meeting because they were knowledgeable community leaders and were interested in the ultimate success of the project. The facilitator reminded them why they were there and what they had to accomplish. He summarized the steps of the NGT process and then passed out a sheet of paper to each person with the following question at the top of the page: What are the criteria that should be met in order to assure that the community meeting is truly representative?

He gave the group four minutes to jot down ideas in response to that question. He made it clear that he would not be picking up the papers, but that they were worksheets for group members to use as they saw fit. After the time was up, he went around the table and asked each of the participants to contribute one criterion, which he wrote on newsprint. As he filled each sheet of newsprint, he taped it to the wall so that it could be viewed by the whole group. The group generated 18 criteria.

The facilitator then read each criterion in order and asked the group to question any of the criteria that were not clear to them. After that serial discussion, which led to a consolidation of a few of the criteria, a voting procedure was used to identify which of the criteria the group thought were most important. First, they each selected what they thought were the five most important criteria and wrote each of them on separate 3 × 5 cards. Second, they were led through a procedure that allowed each of them to rank-order their five preferences. All of the cards were collected and tallied. A discussion of the vote resulted in the group's agreement on what should be the criteria.

After a break, the group was asked to take about ten minutes and to write down on a sheet of paper the names of people who met the criteria and would make a substantial contribution to the community meeting. While the group was working silently and independently, the facilitator placed single sheets of paper on the wall with one criteria on each sheet. When the ten minutes were up, he passed out large index cards to each of the participants. As he called upon each of the participants, he asked them to recommend a name, to print the name on one of the index cards, and to suggest which of the criteria that person met. He then taped the recommended name on the wall beneath the appropriate criterion.

After the names were up on the wall, the group discussed the suitability of the list. They suggested additional names where there appeared to be gaps and reduced the number where there were too many in a category.

The meeting ended with each person present being assigned different responsibilities (such as arranging for the meeting site, drafting the letter of invitation, contacting certain potential participants, and mailing out the invitations) for conducting the community meeting.

One of the decisions made at the planning meeting was that NGT would be a suitable process to use at the community meeting in order to enable the citizens to identify the needs of the community. The facilitator determined that it would be most productive if local citizens ran the NGT sessions at the community meeting. Therefore, a training session was planned in order to prepare selected citizens to play that role.

The training session, held the day before the community meeting, lasted two hours. Eight persons learned how to conduct an NGT by participating in a session that simulated what would be done the following day. They even used the same NGT question, which provided an opportunity to test whether or not the question elicited the desired results. After the simulated session, the facilitator debriefed the prospective group leaders.

The community meeting began with presentations on why the group was meeting and what were some of the critical issues facing the region. Seven groups, with 9 to 14 members each, used NGT to address the following question: What issues, problems, and opportunities should be addressed in order to make the region a better place to live in the 1980s? (This appears to be a complex question rather than the preferred simple question. However, it was explained to those in attendance that they may have different orientations; some may think in terms of issues, others in terms of problems, and others may see issues or problems as opportunities. The purpose of the small group sessions was to capture all of their ideas.)

During a lunch break, the NGT group leaders met in order to create a composite list of the items that had a high priority in each of the separate groups. When the full group reconvened, the composite list was presented. Members discussed each of the items (for purposes of clarification), modified the language of some of the items, and added items that they thought had priority in their small group but had been left off of the composite list.

They then voted on which of the items on the composite list should have priority.

A report was prepared and distributed to all of those who attended the meeting. The ideas generated at the community meeting became the input for additional planning meetings and substantially influenced what were designated as the priorities in planning for the region.

LIMITATIONS

NGT is easy to learn and use. Moreover, groups enjoy participating in an NGT because they realize they have been unusually productive in a relatively brief time. Consequently, the technique is seductive. Because it is easy to use and accomplishes a great deal, there is a tendency to overuse it. After a while, all problems seem as if they can be addressed by NGT. As one of its benefits is its novelty—groups are "tricked" into being more productive than they would be if they did not use the technique—repeated use may have a dampening effect on a participant.

NGT may also be used in ways that are inappropriate. The technique is not suitable for all questions and all groupings of people. People accustomed to getting their way in groups, including highly verbal people like some politicians, may even resist participation in an NGT. Once they realize they cannot control the outcome as they are accustomed to doing, they are likely to try and modify the process. They will claim that NGT is a "game" or "sophomoric." Those accustomed to being assisted by staff may also be uncomfortable about participation in an NGT.

NGT includes a voting procedure and, therefore, gives the impression that the final product represents a group consensus. The NGT vote may be final—the group might act according to the vote—but usually the principal outcome is the generation of ideas. The vote is simply a way to bring closure to the group's activity and does suggest the group's preferences. The vote is helpful when there are multiple groups (and there is a desire to consolidate the high-priority ideas from each of the groups) or when there is a plan to use another technique—such as Ideawriting, Delphi, or ISM—to develop the ideas suggested by NGT.

Although the ideas generated in an NGT are more developed than those that emerge during a simple brainstorming session, they are still only suggestive. In fact, the product of an NGT session is not usually clear to an external audience that did not participate in the session. Moreover, the quality of the ideas is likely to vary greatly. Some may be shallow, uninformed, or impractical. Therefore, NGT is usually a starting place and needs to be used in conjunction with a technique for idea development.

The following statement was made in response to the ideas that emerged out of the community meeting example presented above. It illustrates the tentative nature of the ideas produced by one NGT conference. Recall that the ideas from a number of NGT sessions were consolidated into a single list and considered by the full group. The NGT question was: "What issues, problems, and opportunities should be addressed in order to make the region a better place to live in the 1980's?"

> The goals as developed were at a very general level. They actually mixed together *topics* (e.g., community planning) with *solutions* (e.g., a new rural water system) with *questions* (e.g., how can we get the Feds to change ill-fitting policies?). More importantly, general statements tend to mask differences. When they become more specific, general concepts which we all favor (such as low-income housing and abundant clean water) can lead to many different perceptions about what is really needed to make individuals happy. In the process of specifying concrete objectives, it is also important to make clear the *relationship* between a problem and a solution. In many programs, they are not as tightly connected as they need to be. (Williams, 1980, p. A1)

This limitation is a principal reason why participants in an NGT session need to understand how the NGT product will be used. If possible, the participants need to be apprised of the full project and how their participation fits within the project.

Time is usually a constraint on a group, and that influences the NGT steps. The goal of Step 3 is to clarify ideas. The relative merit of the ideas could be discussed and argued, but that takes considerably more time. Moreover, it is likely to put the group into an interacting mode and allow some people to dominate the proceedings. However, if it is necessary (or even appropriate) for the group to consider the relative merit of the ideas, schedule sufficient time for that to occur.

RESOURCES

Nominal Group Technique was invented in 1968 by Andre Delbecq and Andrew Van de Ven. The most comprehensive description can be found in Delbecq et al. (1975). Delbecq and Sandra Gill have a chapter on NGT in Olsen (1982).

APPENDIX 3.1

SUMMARY OF NGT PROCEDURES

Premeeting Preparation

(1) Formulate and test the NGT question.
(2) Assemble supplies.
(3) Prepare the meeting room.
(4) Train inexperienced group leaders.

Opening Statement

Inform the participants of the context of the session, indicating how NGT results will be used in subsequent steps. Summarize the four basic NGT steps.

Conducting the NGT Process

(1) Silent Generation of Ideas in Writing
Read the question aloud and ask members to list their responses in phrases or brief sentences. Request that they work silently and independently. Allow 4 to 8 minutes.

(2) Round-Robin Recording of Ideas
Go around the table and get one idea from each member. Write the ideas on a large flip-chart. As you finish each sheet, tape it on the wall so that the entire list is visible. Encourage hitchhiking on other ideas. Do not allow discussion, elaboration, or justification.

(3) Serial Discussion of the List of Ideas
Explain that the purpose of this step is clarification. Read item 1 aloud and invite comments. Then read item 2, and continue discussing each item in turn until the list is covered. Arguments are unnecessary because each member will have a chance to vote independently in Step 4. As soon as the logic of a position is clear, cut off discussion.

(4) Voting
Each person selects the five (or more) items that are most important to him or her and writes each on a 3 × 5 card. These are then rank-

ordered. The votes are recorded on the flip-chart in front of the group. The group then discusses the voting patterns. If desired, the items can be further clarified and a second vote taken.

* * *

APPENDIX 3.2

The following is a partial example of *how to present the results of a typical NGT session.*

NGT question: What issues, problems, and opportunities should be addressed in order to make the region a better place to live in the 1980s?

Votes	Items
2, 1, 1, 1	(1) Maintain and develop natural and human resources; creation of industry and jobs.
	(2) Development of educational resources: funding base, curriculum, facilities.
5, 4, 5, 5, 3, 4	(3) Reduce dependency on federal funds; develop own resources.
3, 2	(4) Adequate water treatment and sewage facilities.
5	(5) County government underfunded.
	(6) Strong program to induce pro business legislation and reform. Effect change in political process.

3

Ideawriting

This chapter describes Ideawriting and includes sections on premeeting preparations, the opening statement, conducting the Ideawriting process, and analyzing and reporting the Ideawriting product. Two examples of Ideawriting, along with sections on limitations and resources, are also included.

Ideawriting, a group method for developing ideas and exploring their meaning, is particularly helpful in making more specific the general ideas that result from group interactions. Another valuable use of Ideawriting is idea generation.

Ideawriting typically includes four steps:

(1) Group organization: A large group is divided into small working groups.
(2) Initial response: Each participant reacts in writing to a stimulus question or item and then places his or her pad (with the initial response) in the center of the group.
(3) Written interaction: Each participant reacts, in writing, to what is written on each of the other pads.
(4) Analysis and reporting: Each participant reads the comments made in reaction to his or her initial response, the small working group discusses the principal ideas that emerge from the written interaction, and the group summarizes the discussion on newsprint.

Ideawriting focuses on a single topic, requires a relatively brief time, and produces a written product. The process recognizes that (1) certain group goals can be achieved best by writing rather than by discussion; (2) parallel working (each of the members of the group work on the same task at the same time) is productive and efficient; and (3) all members of a group should be allowed an equal opportunity to express their ideas. The process is quite useful when the group is large, the meeting schedule allocates a limited time for group discussion, or differences among group members (in status and verbal aggressiveness) need to be neutralized.

An important advantage of Ideawriting is that one leader can facilitate the work of a large number of Ideawriting groups. This means that the technique is useful for larger conferences or meetings. An Ideawriting session can easily be accomplished in an hour, and an abbreviated version in a half-hour.

> CAUTION: Do not use Ideawriting unless the participants are willing to express themselves in writing. The legibility of the writing is not usually an issue, but if participants are self-conscious about their ability to express themselves in writing, they may not cooperate or they may even disrupt the process.

PREMEETING PREPARATIONS

First, decide whether the group task requires that all members respond to the same stimulus, such as a common question, or whether members should select the item they prefer from a list of alternatives.

If a single triggering question is used as the stimulus to the group activity, formulate and if possible test the question. An example of an appropriate question would be, "What is an effective strategy for generating additional jobs in the private sector?"

If the group members are to respond to a set of stimulus items, write those items on newsprint so that they can be displayed before the group. For example, the group might have a previously prepared list of potential strategies for generating additional jobs in the private sector. If so, write the list on sheets of newsprint and tape them to the wall. The question for this group might be, "What are critical considerations that must be taken into account in implementing any one of the potential strategies?"

Second, assemble necessary supplies: pads of paper, pencils, pens, tables, and chairs. If the groups are to analyze and report their results, at least one flip-chart (or easel), newsprint, masking tape, and felt-tip pens should also be available. Each Ideawriting group should have a separate table around which to sit.

OPENING STATEMENT

Briefly,

(1) Stress the importance of the task.
(2) State how the results will be used.
(3) Summarize the basic steps of the Ideawriting process. Present the steps on a sheet of newsprint and/or on the Ideawriting sheets.
(4) Special reminders:
    (a) Note that the writing should be done silently.
    (b) Tell the participants not to worry about their writing (style, spelling, or punctuation). Suggest that they may write in phrases, rather than sentences. The emphasis is on ideas, not wording.
    (c) Explain that the sheets should not be torn off the pads; sets of comments should remain together.
    (d) Observe that the silent writing phase should be completed in 15 to 20 minutes.

CONDUCTING THE IDEAWRITING PROCESS

Group Organization

If the group is large, divide it into small groups of three to six persons. The ideal size is three or four.

Ask one person in each small group to serve as the group leader. Charge the leaders with the responsibility of seeing to it that the groups follow the steps of the process. In a very large group, you might ask them to count off and then designate all the number "ones" as leaders. The key is to have someone responsible in each group for an orderly expeditious process.

Initial Response

If the group is responding to a triggering question, members should write their names in the upper right-hand corner, write the triggering question at the top of a page of their pads, and briefly list their responses to the question (see Figure 3.1).

IDEAWRITING

NAME:

ITEM:

INSTRUCTIONS:

1. Step one: Initial response

Using this worksheet, each participant should:
- write his or her name in the space at the top of this page,
- take 5 to 10 minutes to respond to the ITEM by writing in the RESPONSE section below, and
- work quickly, silently, and independently.

2. Step two: Written interaction

- After completing the initial RESPONSE to the ITEM, and after all of the worksheets have been placed in the center of the table, each participant should select a worksheet other than his or her own, read it, and react to it by writing additional comments.
- This process should be repeated until everyone has responded to every other person's ideas.

RESPONSE:

Figure 3.1 Ideawriting Page with Instructions

If the group is responding to a set of stimulus items (e.g., sheets of newsprint on the wall with strategies), members should write their names in the upper right-hand corner, select and write one item (e.g., one of the strategies), and write their responses to the item. It may be useful to assign items. Otherwise, let each member select whichever item interests him or her the most. This alternative may result in duplicate items, but experience suggests that a variety of ideas will be developed.

Written Interaction

Members should place their pads in the center of the table. They should select a pad other than their own and briefly respond to what is on the paper by adding written comments below the original material. It is appropriate to offer solutions, qualify what is written, add suggestions, and criticize weaknesses.

Each person should return the pad to the center of the table. Repeat this process until each member has responded to every other member's ideas.

ANALYZING AND REPORTING
THE IDEAWRITING PRODUCT

The process may now be considered complete. If so, analysis of the Ideawriting sheets will be left to a monitoring team and reported at a later date.

The group may want to analyze and report the product of the Ideawriting process immediately. If so, the following steps should be followed:

- Members should read the comments on their pads and orally report them for the other members of their small group. The ideas can then be discussed and summarized.
- It is advisable that each of the small groups summarize its efforts on a single sheet of newsprint as the sheets provide an efficient way to report back to the large group once it reconvenes.
- The group should appoint one of its members (perhaps the assigned group leader) to report the general findings of the group's work to the large group.
- At the large group session, the representatives from each small group should report on the group's ideas, perhaps by explaining the sheet of newsprint.
- The large group can then discuss the ideas.

AN EXAMPLE

A mayor appointed a task force of 15 persons to recommend actions that city government and local business firms could take to cope with a chronically high unemployment rate. Having decided to use Idea-writing as a method for generating and refining recommendations, the chairperson prepared for the first meeting by drafting a triggering question to which everyone would respond: What can the public and private sectors in this community do to reduce unemployment?

When the task force convened, the chairperson explained the purpose of the group and how the mayor was likely to use its report. The chairperson read the question and proposed Ideawriting as the best way to tap the experience and judgment of every member. After describing the process and securing the group's agreement to try it, the chairperson divided the task force into three five-member groups. Someone in each group was asked to make sure that the Ideawriting proceeded smoothly.

Each group sat around a small table, out of earshot of the others. The few last-minute questions about the process were briefly discussed and clarified. Then a silent writing phase began.

Individually, group members wrote their last names and the triggering question at the top of the first page of a pad of paper. Next, everyone responded to the question by writing a few ideas. Members were free to respond in any way they wished. Some provided short lists of alternatives; others described the important characteristics of a single action. One person stated why, in his judgment, the group was dealing with the wrong question.

After the initial response, members placed their pads in the center of the table, took the pad of another group member, read what the other had written, and wrote a few comments in response. Again, a wide variety of responses were made. Many members were stimulated to add new alternative actions. Some identified potential problems with other members' suggestions or pointed out how a particular proposal could be implemented. Still others indicated which of the suggested actions had the greatest promise in the short run.

The process of alternatively reading and writing ideas continued in silence until each person had commented on the ideas of all other group members. When the originators got their pads back, they contained five brief statements, only the first of which was written by them. In

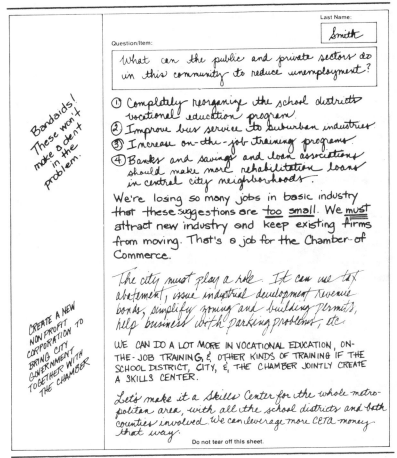

Figure 3.2 Sample Ideawriting Page

this fashion, each of the small groups produced five sets of suggested actions, as well as critiques of those actions. A pad looked something like Figure 3.2.

After the silent writing was over, members read what was on their pads and summarized them orally for the rest of the group. The group discussed and synthesized the major ideas, writing them on a sheet of newsprint. The task force reconvened to hear reports from all three groups. The chairperson used the newsprint summaries to assign topics to committees for additional study.

ANOTHER EXAMPLE

The following example illustrates one of the advantages of Idea-writing—that one person can facilitate the work of a large number of people.

Approximately 700 people participated in an Ideawriting session at an international conference. The purpose of the session (to introduce the participants to techniques that are useful for thinking about the future, as well as to generate some ideas on a particular topic) and the steps in the process were briefly outlined at a general assembly for all of the participants. The full group then subdivided into four groups. The participants in the four groups sat at tables with approximately 8 to 10 persons per table. Three common activities were followed by each table:

(1) The tables established subgroups of 4 to 5 persons per group.
(2) Each subgroup was assigned a goal. The following are examples of the goals they were assigned.
   (a) Reduce Energy Consumption
   (b) Use Public Sector Resources More Efficiently
   (c) Provide a Range of Public Community Facilities.
(3) Each subgroup used Ideawriting in the following manner.
   (a) They placed their stimulus question at the top of their Ideawriting pad. An example would be, "How can we plan and construct build-ings and development projects so that we *reduce energy con-sumption?*" The question was the same for everyone, only the goals (e.g., reduce energy consumption) differed.
   (b) Ten minutes were allotted for each participant to independently respond to the question.
   (c) Twenty minutes were allotted for the participants to engage in written interaction. Each of them selected a pad other than his or her own, read it, and reacted to it by writing additional comments. The process was repeated until everyone had responded to every other person's ideas.
   (d) Each subgroup summarized their Ideawriting work by having each individual read the sheet he or she initiated and then by dis-cussing the ideas. Each table identified the five most promising options, ideas, characteristics, or plans.

(e) Each table then completed one IMPACT ANALYSIS matrix (Figure 3.3) by
- filling in, across the top of the matrix, the five most promising options,
- making a group judgment (a show of hands was sufficient) about the extent to which each option facilitated the achievement of each the goals. They used the following symbols:
    + = beneficial impact
    − = detrimental impact
    ↗ = uncertain or mixed impact
    0 = no likely impact, and
- completing each box in the matrix by circling the most applicable of the four symbols.

(f) Each table then examined the matrix in order to identify those options that seemed to have a beneficial impact on most of the goals.

A spokesperson for each of the four groups reported to the general assembly when the full group reconvened. The Ideawriting process, including filling in the IMPACT ANALYSIS, took approximately 90 minutes.

One person facilitated the work in each of the four rooms, so that there were four facilitators for 700 participants.

LIMITATIONS

As the demands of facilities and supplies are not great, there are few limitations on the use of Ideawriting. The principal limitation would be the group that is participating in the process; it is imperative that they be willing to express themselves in writing. One should not be hesitant about using Ideawriting with a group of professionals, but should be cautious about using the process with a group of citizens or even elected officials. These groups may be suitable, but the burden falls on the group leader to make that assessment.

RESOURCES

There are few printed references to Ideawriting, other than John Warfield (1976), who refers to it as "brainwriting," and Thissen, Sage, and Warfield (1980).

IMPACT ANALYSIS

INSTRUCTIONS:

+	= beneficial impact
−	= detrimental impact
✓	= uncertain or mixed impact
0	= no likely impact

Each table should complete one IMPACT ANALYSIS matrix by doing the following:
Ø Fill in, across the top of the matrix, the 5 most promising OPTIONS identified by your group.
Ø Make a group judgment about the extent to which each OPTION facilitates the achievement of each of the GOALS. Use the symbols +, -, ✓, and 0 (defined at left).
Ø Complete each box in the matrix below for each GOAL by circling the most applicable of the four symbols.

Fill in the OPTIONS → ⌐GOALS	OPTION 1	OPTION 2	OPTION 3	OPTION 4	OPTION 5
A. Reduce Energy Consumption	+ − ✓ 0	+ − ✓ 0	+ − ✓ 0	+ − ✓ 0	+ − ✓ 0
B. Use Public Sector Resources More Efficiently	+ − ✓ 0	+ − ✓ 0	+ − ✓ 0	+ − ✓ 0	+ − ✓ 0
C. Provide a Range of Public Community Facilities	+ − ✓ 0	+ − ✓ 0	+ − ✓ 0	+ − ✓ 0	+ − ✓ 0
D. Use Private Sector Resources More Carefully	+ − ✓ 0	+ − ✓ 0	+ − ✓ 0	+ − ✓ 0	+ − ✓ 0
E. Facilitate Economic Development	+ − ✓ 0	+ − ✓ 0	+ − ✓ 0	+ − ✓ 0	+ − ✓ 0
F. Contain Housing and Development Costs	+ − ✓ 0	+ − ✓ 0	+ − ✓ 0	+ − ✓ 0	+ − ✓ 0
G. Facilitate Social and Economic Mobility	+ − ✓ 0	+ − ✓ 0	+ − ✓ 0	+ − ✓ 0	+ − ✓ 0
H. Meet the Needs of Diverse Households	+ − ✓ 0	+ − ✓ 0	+ − ✓ 0	+ − ✓ 0	+ − ✓ 0
I. Provide a High Level of Private Amenities	+ − ✓ 0	+ − ✓ 0	+ − ✓ 0	+ − ✓ 0	+ − ✓ 0
J. Maintain the Benefits of Accessibility	+ − ✓ 0	+ − ✓ 0	+ − ✓ 0	+ − ✓ 0	+ − ✓ 0
K. Maintain Private Sector Motivation	+ − ✓ 0	+ − ✓ 0	+ − ✓ 0	+ − ✓ 0	+ − ✓ 0
L. Maintain Existing Environmental Standards	+ − ✓ 0	+ − ✓ 0	+ − ✓ 0	+ − ✓ 0	+ − ✓ 0

ACP/5-5-80

Figure 3.3 Impact Analysis Page with Instructions

APPENDIX 3.1

SUMMARY OF THE STEPS
IN THE IDEAWRITING PROCESS

(1) Group Organization
(2) Initial Response
   - Write down a few ideas in response to a stimulus item and then place the pad in the center of the table.
   - Work quickly, silently, independently.
   - Do not tear the sheet off the pad; additional sheets need to be left for others to use.
(3) Written Interaction
   - After the pads with the initial reactions have been placed in the center of the table, select another member's pad, read it, and briefly respond by writing additional comments.
   - Repeat this process until each member has responded to every other person's ideas.
(4) Analysis and Reporting
   - Analysis of the sheets will be left to a monitoring team, in which case the process is complete.
      OR
   - If immediate analysis is desired, each small group discusses its products. The group summarizes its efforts on a single sheet of newsprint and the summaries are shared at a large group session.

4

Delphi Technique and the Mail Questionnaire

This chapter describes types of the Delphi Technique and provides three extended examples of its use. The chapter also describes the ten stages of a mail questionnaire, the choices that have to be made at each of the stages, and makes recommendations regarding which choice is most likely to enhance a high response rate. In addition to providing a time table for administering a mail questionnaire, the chapter includes sections on limitations, lessons, and resources.

The Delphi Technique was devised in the early 1950s in order to enable a group at the Rand Corporation to answer a question posed by the Air Force: "How many A-bombs of the type that destroyed Hiroshima would it take to cut the U.S. gross national product by 75 percent?" The rationale for the Delphi Technique, according to one of its founders, is "that 'n' heads are better than one. It is logical that if you properly combine the judgment of a large number of people, you have a better chance of getting closer to the truth" (Helmer, 1981, p. 83).

One of Delphi's principal uses has been to make future projections and forecasts. Named for the Oracles at Delphi, Greece, who would forecast future events, the technique was first used as a means of prediction and many of its developers and users look upon it as a forecasting tool. Delphi also can be used to

- identify goals and objectives,
- array possible alternatives,
- establish priorities,
- reveal group values,
- gather information, and
- educate a respondent group.

Delphi is useful whenever it is desirable to have pooled judgment.

The Delphi Technique uses a series of questionnaires to aggregate the knowledge, judgments, or opinions of experts (who are usually

anonymous) in order to address complex questions. Individual contributions are shared with the whole group by using the results from
each questionnaire to construct the next questionnaire.

An expert is someone who possesses the knowledge or experience
necessary to participate in a Delphi. A nuclear physicist is an appropriate expert if the Delphi concerns atomic energy and a resident of
a neighborhood is an expert on what should be a community's goals.

TYPES OF DELPHI

In a *conventional* Delphi,

> A small monitor team designs a questionnaire which is sent to a larger
> respondent group. After the questionnaire is returned the monitor team
> summarizes the results and, based upon the results, develops a new ques
> tionnaire for the respondent group. The respondent group is usually given
> at least one opportunity to reevaluate its original answers based upon
> examination of the group response (Linstone & Turoff, 1975, p. 5).

A *real-time* Delphi differs from the conventional Delphi in that,
rather than taking weeks to conduct the process, it occurs during the
course of a meeting or a computer conference. The respondents are
likely to be attending the meeting or are connected by means of computer terminals so the time for distribution and collection of questionnaires is minimized. Moreover, the questionnaires are likely to be
designed so that analysis of the responses can be done efficiently, often
with the assistance of a computer or data processor.

The objectives of a *policy* Delphi are "to ensure that all possible
options have been put on the table for consideration, to estimate the
impact and consequences of any particular option, and to examine and
estimate the acceptability of any particular option" (Turoff, 1975,
p. 87). It is based on the premise

> that the decisionmaker is not interested in having a group generate his
> decision; but rather, have an informed group present all the options and
> supporting evidence for his consideration. The Policy Delphi is...not
> a mechanism for making decisions. Generating a consensus is not the
> prime objective (Turoff, 1975, p. 84).

According to Turoff (1975, p. 88), the following are the phases in the communication process of a Policy Delphi:

(1) Formulation of the issues: What is the issue that really should be under consideration? How should it be stated?

(2) Exposing the options: Given the issues, what are the policy options available?

(3) Determining initial positions on the issues: Which are the ones everyone already agrees upon and which are the unimportant ones to be discarded? Which are the ones exhibiting disagreement among the respondents?

(4) Exploring and obtaining the reasons for disagreements: What underlying assumptions, views, or facts are being used by the individuals to support their respective positions?

(5) Evaluating the underlying reasons: How does the group view the separate arguments used to defend various positions, and how do they compare to one another on a relative basis?

(6) Reevaluating the options: Reevaluation is based upon the views of the underlying "evidence" and the assessment of its relevance to each position taken.

In order that the policy Delphi take three or four rounds, rather than the five rounds that would be necessary to accomplish all six communication phases, the monitor team needs to formulate the first questionnaire. That is often done by reviewing pertinent literature, interviewing informed persons, or using a technique like NGT or Idea-writing to ascertain the views of a group.

Linstone and Turoff (1975, p. 4) have identified criteria that can be used to determine when Delphi should be used. A Delphi is useful when

- [a] problem does not lend itself to precise analytical techniques but can benefit from subjective judgments on a collective basis,
- the individuals needed to contribute to the examination of a broad or complex problem have no history of adequate communication and may represent diverse backgrounds with respect to experience or expertise,
- more individuals are needed than can effectively interact in a face-to-face exchange,
- time and cost make frequent group meetings infeasible,
- the efficiency of face-to-face meetings can be increased by a supplemental group communication process,

- disagreements among individuals are so severe or politically unpalatable that the communication process must be refereed and/or anonymity assured,
- the heterogeneity of the participants must be preserved to assure validity of the results, i.e., avoidance of domination by quantity or by strength of personality ("bandwagon effect"). [In other words, use Delphi if it is necessary to have diverse participants and if you believe that the number of participants or the personalities of particular participants would interfere with equal and effective participation by all of the selected respondents.]

The reason for the compound title to this chapter—"Delphi Technique and the Mail Questionnaire"—is that the questionnaire is the essential tool in the Delphi, but there are likely to be many occasions when applied researchers will want to use a *single* mail questionnaire in conjunction with one of the other techniques presented in this book. In those instances, it would not be accurate to call the questionnaire a Delphi, as feedback by means of *repeated iterations* is inherent to the nature of a Delphi.

AN EXAMPLE

A researcher (Cooper, 1977) wanted to know whether his academic discipline could make a contribution toward solving critical societal problems, so he set out to discover which contemporary and future societal problems were amenable to treatment and ultimate solution using inputs from the field of speech communications.

He determined that the essential technique he would use to answer the question would be Delphi. In order to decide who would participate in the Delphi, he arranged for an NGT session. Five speech communication professors were asked to identify individuals in their discipline who would meet certain criteria. They identified 45 potential participants. All 45 were contacted, and 33 agreed to participate in the study.

The Delphi consisted of three rounds. The first questionnaire included an inventory of contemporary and future societal problems that were gleaned from the literature. The respondents were asked whether they agreed with the inventory, would add items to it, or would revise items. The goal of the second round was to prioritize the problems in the refined inventory, which was created as a result of the responses to the first questionnaire. The respondents identified the relative importance of each of the items.

The goal of the third round was to reveal how the priority societal problems were related to one another and to determine which current and future resources of the speech communication field could be applied toward the solution of priority problems.

When the study was completed, the researcher had identified what a community of scholars believed were priority societal problems (they identified the following problems, listed in order of importance: (1) potential for mass destruction; (2) nuclear weapons, control by governments, potential access by small groups and individuals; (3) water pollution; (4) malnutrition and famine; (5) alternatives to fossil fuel; (6) growth of armaments worldwide; (7) unemployment; (8) inflation; and (9) air pollution [Cooper, 1977, p. 50]), what was the interdependence of the problems, and what were the resources of their discipline that might have some bearing on resolving the problems.

One example of a communication resource that is currently available to address the problem of inflation is persuasion theory, which is related to the problem in that "one of the major causes of inflation is psychological; the confidence and belief of the public and the shaping of their behavior are critical for control of inflation. [Persuasion theory is a] means for mass influence of economic practices and economic negotiation" (Cooper, 1977, p. 84). A new resource that is likely to be available in the future is a "knowledge of communication principles for dissemination of technical information." That will be helpful, because a "widespread understanding of economic data, principles, and policies are essential to control inflation" (Cooper, 1977, p. 84).

The appendix at the end of this chapter includes samples of the instruments used to conduct this Delphi study.

ANOTHER EXAMPLE

Another researcher (Sorensen, 1982) asked, "What are the communication problems of the aged in one county and what policy options exist to address them?" To answer the question, he conducted a series of NGTs and a Delphi.

NGTs were held with the local commission on aging, faculty and students at the local university, a Golden Kiwanis Club, nurses, social service personnel, senior citizen center directors, and elderly residents. The product of the NGTs was combined with a review of the literature on the communication needs of the aged in order to identify 103 possible problems or needs. In turn, these were combined in order to produce the first questionnaire.

The Delphi consisted of three rounds. The goal of the first round, to identify those particular problems and needs that were most relevant to the residents of the county, was achieved by sending the questionnaire to a diverse group of residents. The respondents were asked whether or not they agreed that each item was an important problem in the community.

The second-round questionnaire asked the respondents to rate the priority of the "most important" problems (based on the results of the first round). Space was provided for the respondents to add problems or needs that had not been included.

The purpose of the third round was to solicit what the respondents thought would be solutions for the high-priority problems. Space was provided so the respondents could write in solutions for the 21 highest-priority problems.

The outcome of the study was that a number of problems and needs were identified, along with possible solutions for addressing them. The results were given to those who were responsible for making policy related to the elderly in the community.

ANOTHER EXAMPLE

The first two examples illustrate how Delphi was used in order to tap the knowledge and opinions of two different communities: a community of scholars and a group of citizens (along with the support structure and professionals who serve them). The following example is of a rather simple Delphi, used between two planning meetings in order to complete work that was left undone at the first meeting.

Scholars and practitioners served together on an advisory committee to a group of engineers. The engineers were preparing a document for a national foundation. At one of the advisory committee meetings, a variety of reactions and suggestions were offered regarding the nature, preparation, and distribution of the document. However, there was not sufficient time at the close of the meeting in order for the members of the committee to clearly phrase priorities and reach consensus regarding their suggestions for changing the document.

A questionnaire was prepared that distributed an unedited list of suggestions to the full advisory committee and asked them to (1) rephrase any of the items so that they would be clear and (2) suggest additional changes that ought to be made in the proposed document. The responses to the questionnaire enabled the construction of a second questionnaire.

A second questionnaire was prepared and sent to each committee member. Round two asked them to rate the importance of each of the suggested changes. Based on the responses to round two, a report was prepared that identified changes that were very important and had to be made if the document was to be used as intended. A second set of suggestions fell into the category of items that were important and ought to be done to strengthen the document. A third group fell under the category of suggestions that were somewhat important; they might be done to strengthen the document. A fourth group the respondents did not support at all, and they did not need to be done. The monitoring team prepared an interpretation of the results. The engineers responsible for preparing the document adapted many of the suggestions and felt that they were able to prepare a stronger document as a result of having received such clear advice.

MAIL QUESTIONNAIRE

The essential tool of a Delphi, a mail questionnaire, includes at least *ten stages.*

    (1) Decide to administer questionnaire.
    (2) Select a respondent group.
    (3) Design the questionnaire.
    (4) Give advance notice to respondents (optional).
    (5) Pilot test questionnaire (optional).
    (6) Produce questionnaire.
    (7) Distribute questionnaire.
    (8) Send reminder or another copy of the questionnaire (optional).
    (9) Receive completed questionnaires.
  (10) Analyze completed questionnaires.

The researcher has to make choices at each of these stages. The choices are listed below. Following each of the choices, and in italics, are recommendations. The recommendations are based on a review of the literature on designing mail questionnaires, my own experiences, and the assumptions of Delphi: (1) that respondents are selected because they are expert on the subject (there are no nonexperts, only poorly designed studies), and (2) that the purpose is to pool judgments and/or give advice, *not* to generalize about a population.

Recommendations are offered in order to suggest what is most likely to enhance a high response rate. The tradeoff that precludes simply recommending the ideal option in each instance is between maximizing the return and minimizing the cost. Many of the recommendations are tempered by the resources that are available to execute the study. Recommendations cannot be offered for some choices because they are so situational.

Stages	*Choices*
(1) Decide to administer questionnaire.	(1.a) Should you use a mail questionnaire or some other method to collect data?

Recommendation: Utilize a mail questionnaire if at least one of the following criteria are critical:

- *It is desirable to assure the anonymity of the participants.*
- *The respondents are more likely to respond to a mail questionnaire than to an opportunity to participate in a meeting and/or agree to a personal interview.*
- *The respondents are separated by a substantial distance, and costs prohibit holding a meeting or interviewing each respondent.*
- *The respondent group is too large to be queried in any other fashion.*

(2) Select respondent group.	(2.a) What is the population you want to study?

The Delphi asks you to decide which individuals or groups have the knowledge, judgment, and/or opinions that are needed.

> (2.b) What is the sample you want to study?
>   (2.b.1) How large a sample do you need?

Rules of thumb: homogeneous population = 15-30; heterogeneous population = 5-10 per category.

(2.b.2) How should you select the sample?

Nomination by the monitoring team and/or advisory group.

(3) Design questionnaire.   (3.a) What should the cover letter be like?
                              (3.a.1) Who should be listed as the sponsor/source?

If you have choices, whoever will have the most credibility with the respondent group.

(3.a.2) Should the letter be personalized (personally addressed to each respondent)?

Yes. (Note: This recommendation, like many that follow, needs to be considered in light of the available resources, including technology and time. The "yes" means that if the resources are available—for example, a computer with mailmerge—this should be done as it is likely to enhance response.)

(3.a.2.a) Should each letter be signed individually?

Yes.

(3.a.2.b) Should each letter be produced individually?

Yes.

(3.a.3) What appeal(s) should be utilized?

Those that are appropriate for the respondent group. These might be their interest in the subject, the way the results will be used, their unique ability to make a contribution to the study.

(3.a.4) Should an incentive be offered?
(3.a.4.a) Should a premium be offered?

Yes. Keep it small: a pencil or pen that can be used to complete the questionnaire(s), a small amount of money (like a quarter). The research suggests that a premium enhances returns, but that a larger premium does not realize a larger return.

(3.a.4.b) Should the respondents be offered a copy of the questionnaire results?

Yes. Do not ask if they want a copy of the results. If they are appropriate respondents, they will want to see the results. Announce in the cover letter that you will send them a copy. (And keep your word!)

(3.b) Is demographic information needed about the respondents?
(3.b.1) Should the respondents be asked to provide demographic information?

Usually No, as it can conflict with the cardinal principle of assuring anonymity.

(3.b.2) What demographic information should be requested?

Do not ask for name, address, or other information that will identify the respondent. If demographic information is needed, perhaps due to the diversity of the respondents, only ask for essential information.

(3.b.3) How much demographic information should be requested?

As little as is necessary.

(3.b.4) At what point in the questionnaire should demographic information be requested?

*A case can be made for beginning, middle, or end. The end is con-
venient because information can easily be separated from the remainder
of the questionnaire.*

(3.c) Are instructions necessary?
(3.c.1) Should instructions be
included?

*Only if the questionnaire is sufficiently complex to warrant them. If
instructions need to be included, it is beneficial to guide the response
by providing an example. If you want a limited number of responses,
leave a limited number of spaces. Make the instructions clear and
simple.*

(3.c.2) Should the respondents' anonymity be assured?

Yes. And keep your word. No trick coding.

(3.c.2.a) Should the respondents sign the ques-
tionnaire?

*Only if the questionnaire is sufficiently complex to warrant them. If
naire, so additional responses can be encouraged. Two strategies that
can be used to determine who has returned questionnaires (but will
help assure anonymity) are (1) to have a section that can be signed,
cut off, and mailed back, and (2) to include a postcard that can be
signed and returned separately.*

(3.c.3) Should the respondents be
given a deadline?

Yes.

(3.c.3.a) How much time
should the respon-
dents be given to

return the question-
naire?

Ten days from the date you mail, if you send the questionnaire first class. More time if you use bulk mailing, and less time if hand delivered.

(3.d) What is the questionnaire like?

An excellent reference for the design of questionnaires is Dillman (1978). Also see Fowler (1984).

(3.d.1) What should the questions be like?

(3.d.1.a) How should the questions be designed (including the language, length, comprehensibility, clarity?

(3.d.1.b) What types of questions should be used?

(3.d.1.c) What should the opening question be like?

(3.d.1.d) Should there be a "logic" to the order of the questions?

(3.d.1.e) Should the questions be "grouped"?

(3.d.2) Should scales (such as Likert agree/disagree scales) be utilized?

(3.d.3) How long should the questionnaire be?

(4) Give advance notice. (optional)

(4.a) Should the respondents be given advance notice that they will receive the questionnaire?

As brief as possible. Only ask what is essential. Resist seeking responses that would be nice to have but that you do not need.

Yes.

> (4.b) What should be the format of the advance notice?
> (4.b.1) Should it be a letter?
> (4.b.2) Should it be a postcard?
> (4.b.3) Should it be a telephone call?
> (4.b.4) Should it be by personal contact?

First choice: personal contact. Second choice: phone call. Third choice: letter. Fourth choice: postcard.

> (4.c) How much in advance of receiving the questionnaire should the respondents receive advance notice?

Three to seven days.

> (5) Pilot test questionnaire (optional)
> (5.a) Who should be the subjects for a pilot test?

A few people who are like the respondent group.

> (5.b) What should be the process for a pilot test?

Ask participants to complete the questionnaire. Do not provide verbal instructions. Debrief them by asking for their general reactions and then by asking specific questions that you believe could be unclear for the respondents. Questions might be asked after you examine their responses. The pilot could be administered individually or in a group.

The next step, producing the questionnaire, may come before the pilot test. It is included after on the assumption that the pilot test may take the form of a draft of the final version—albeit a good one, so that you get a good test—and that final decisions will be made after you get the results from the pilot test.

> (6) Produce questionnaire.
> (6.a) Should special attention be given to the appearance of the questionnaire?

Yes. See Dillman (1978).

(6.b) What kind of postage should be used on the questionnaire envelope?
(6.b.1) Should it be metered?
(6.b.2) Should it use a regular stamp?
(6.b.3) Should it use a commemorative or special stamp?

First choice: commemorative or special stamp. Second choice: regular stamp. Third choice: metered mail.

(6.c) What arrangements should be made for returning the questionnaire?
(6.c.1) Should it be picked up?
(6.c.2) Should a return envelope be provided?

First choice: pick up. Second choice: provide a stamped return envelope.

(6.c.3) Should there be postage on the return envelope? Should it be metered? Use a regular stamp? Use a commemorative or special stamp?

First choice: commemorative or special stamp. Second choice: regular stamp. Third choice: metered mail.

(7) Distribute questionnaire.

(7.a) Where should the questionnaire be mailed?
(7.a.1) Should the questionnaire be sent to respondents' offices?

Yes.

(7.a.2) Should the questionnaire be sent to respondents' homes?

Normally no. Yes, if a survey of citizens.

          (7.b) Should the questionnaire be hand delivered?

Yes.

          (7.c) Should the questionnaire be published (in the newspaper, an organization's newsletter, etc.)?
              (7.c.1) Should it be published in a newspaper?
              (7.c.2) Should it be published in a magazine?
              (7.c.3) Should it be published in an organizational newsletter?

Only if the results will not be distorted by self-selected responses or if self-selection is not an issue in the study. Publication of the questionnaire may be appropriate for community studies (citizens or scholars) or if the opportunity to participate in the study is one of the goals of the study.

   (8) Send reminder.   (8.a) Should a reminder questionnaire be sent to nonrespondents?

Yes. Particularly if the initial return does not satisfy the goal established for the study and if time permits.

          (8.b) How soon after the mailing of the initial questionnaire should the reminder questionnaire be sent?

Approximately ten days to two weeks depending upon the deadline given in the initial mailing.

          (8.c) What should be the format of the reminder?
              (8.c.1) Should it be a phone call?
              (8.c.2) Should it be a postcard?
              (8.c.3) Should it be a letter?
              (8.c.4) Should it be a personal reminder?

First choice: personal reminder. Second choice: phone call. Third choice: letter. Fourth choice: postcard.

(9) Receive completed
questionnaires.

Use a system for noting that questionnaires have been received.

(10) Analyze completed
questionnaires.

(10.a) How should the questionnaires be tabulated?

(10.b) How should the data be analyzed?

(10.c) How should the results be interpreted?

If a second questionnaire is to be developed, based on the results of the first questionnaire, return to step 3. For the second and all subsequent questionnaires, there is an additional choice at step 7:

(7.d) Who should receive the questionnaire?

(7.d.1) Should all of the initial respondents receive the second (and any subsequent questionnaire?

(7.d.2) Should only those who returned the first questionnaire receive the second questionnaire?

If time, resources, and circumstances permit, all of the initial respondents should receive the second questionnaire. If the kind of learning you would like to achieve or your analysis would be adversely effected, then you should mail only to those who returned the first questionnaire.

Please note that these recommendations do reflect personal preferences. For example, one preference is for personal contact, so the more direct the contact the higher the option is rated. A choice that is less direct, such as postcards, should still bring very satisfactory responses. One value reflected in the recommendations is that the person or team conducting the survey should communicate clearly and honestly with the respondents.

TIME TABLE

Figure 4.1 is a suggested time table for administering a mail questionnaire. It is based on the assumption that the time and resources available to conduct the survey are limited, so there is a need to be as efficient as possible.

LIMITATIONS

A Delphi takes time: One reasonable estimate is 44.5 days (Delbecq et al., 1975, p. 87). Costs will be incurred for supplies, postage, printing, computer time (possibly), personnel to monitor the study, and respondents (if they are compensated for their time or offered a premium).

Critics of the technique believe that a serious limitation is the monitor team responsible for conducting the Delphi. The team could have a bias that may distort the results, abuse the privacy of the respondents, impose too restrictive a process on the participants (e.g., may emphasize consensus to such an extent that useful extreme views are suppressed and conflicts are not resolved), or manipulate the process so that they effect the outcome. Such a potential limitation, however, could be true of most research.

An additional limitation is that Delphi lacks the stimulation of face-to-face communication. According to Delbecq et al. (1975, p. 35), this can lead "to a feeling of detachment from the problem-solving effort" and create "communication and interpretation difficulties among respondents." This can be countered by providing as much personal contact as possible—personal contact when giving advance notice, personally delivering or picking up questionnaires, and so forth.

SOME LESSONS

Delphi does not lend itself to quite the same didactic explication as Nominal Group Technique and Ideawriting: There are many variations possible. What is essential to all the variations is that they include controlled feedback, sequential questionnaires, and assure the anonymity of the respondents.

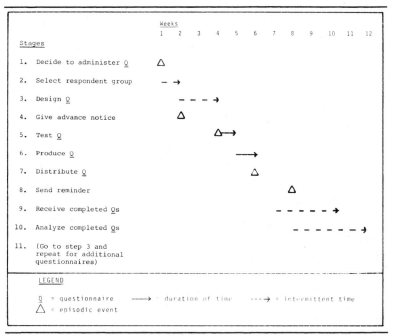

Figure 4.1   Mail Questionnaire Time Table

It is important to establish the credibility of those conducting the Delphi as well as of the process itself. That is often done by conducting the study under the auspices of a sponsor that will be meaningful to the respondents, by making the respondents stakeholders in the study, by identifying the reasons for their selection, and by beginning with a questionnaire (round one) that reveals that the persons conducting the study are knowledgeable about (or at least sensitive to) the subject.

Nominal Group Technique and Ideawriting are useful techniques for "front-ending" the Delphi. One way the monitor team can appear knowledgeable in round one is by gathering their items through the use of these techniques.

The items to which you ask respondents to react should be as concrete as possible. The items will be ineffectual unless they reflect the unique characteristics of the subject or community. The more general the questions are, the less likely it is that they will capture the interest of the respondents.

Quick turn-around time reduces respondent attrition. You keep their attention and motivation if you are able to get the second questionnaire (and all subsequent questionnaires) to them soon after they complete the first one.

Each Delphi round should ask the respondents to perform focused tasks, and preferably one task. It is better to have additional rounds than to complicate an instrument.

It is best to begin with a relatively simple instrument, asking for information that is easy for the respondent to provide (such as filling out scales). The instruments can become more complex once the respondents are committed to the study. Often they will become increasingly more subjective and less quantitative as you move toward collective judgments.

It is part of the very definition of a Delphi that the results from each round dictate the nature of the following round. The nature of all of the rounds cannot be dictated at the outset.

A monitoring team, rather than a single individual, should analyze results and design ensuing rounds.

Delphi is not an end in itself, and the products of Delphis might not be satisfactory in their final form: Often they must be interpreted or used as input into another process for achieving the group's goals.

RESOURCES

Two excellent references on Delphi are Linstone and Turoff (1975) and Delbecq et al. (1975).

APPENDIX 4.1

SAMPLE DELPHI QUESTIONNAIRES

The following samples are taken from the study conducted by Cooper (1977).

The samples include the instructions provided for each round of the study, a sample page from each questionnaire, and the summary of the round two results that were mailed along with the round three questionnaire.

Societal Problems

Delphi: Round 1

The objective of this round is to develop a comprehensive list of contemporary and future societal problems. In preparing for this round the monitoring staff has reviewed the interdisciplinary literature in this area with the intent of preformulating the obvious issues. That review provided the initial range of categories and problems for the inventory on the next page.

Here are the steps we would like you to follow in completing this round's activities:

Instructions

1. Examine the inventory for completeness. If, in your estimation, the list includes the most pressing problems of our day and probable concerns of tomorrow, place a check in the appropriate box at the end of the inventory. Your task is done; return the questionnaire.

2. If you find the inventory to be incomplete, please add the problem(s) which have been omitted in the "Additions" section. If you are uncertain that the issue you envision constitutes a bona fide societal problem, consult the SOCIETAL PROBLEM CRITERIA which is appended to this questionnaire.

3. If any item on the inventory appears to be inaccurate, biased, or otherwise distorted, make a notation to that effect beside the item in the "Comments" column; then, insert your revision in the "Additions" section. Please consider the SOCIETAL PROBLEM CRITERIA prior to making your entries.

WE RECOMMEND ADOPTING A GLOBAL PERSPECTIVE(in contrast to a Speech Communication frame of reference) FOR THE FIRST ROUND. AVAILABLE EVIDENCE SUGGESTS THAT SUCCESSFUL IDENTIFICATION OF PRIORITY PROBLEMS IS NOT DEPENDENT ON A RESPONDENT'S FIELD OF ACADEMIC INTEREST.

PLEASE REFRAIN FROM DELETING ITEMS FROM THE INVENTORY SINCE THIS CAN BE ACCOMPLISHED COLLECTIVELY AND MORE SYSTEMATICALLY IN THE SECOND ROUND.

RETURN THE INVENTORY
IN THE ENVELOPE PROVIDED

Figure 4.2 Round One Instructions

Problem Inventory

PROBLEM   **COMMENTS**

A. <u>War and Peace</u>

   1. Nuclear potential for mass destruction both
   regional and global

   2. Growth of armaments worldwide

   3. War related absorption of resources both
   human and material

   4. Lack of adequate basis for conflict management between nations

B. <u>Population, food, and health</u>

   1. Exponential population growth

   2. Better contraceptive methods: obstacles to
   research, testing, and use

   3. Food production

   4. Food storage and distribution

   5. Malnutrition and famine

   6. Alternative food sources (e.g. ocean farming)

   7. Disease research and cure: cancer, heart-
   stroke, neurological, aging, etc.

   8. Artificial organs and transplants

   9. Psychiatry and mental health: new therapies,
   sanatoriums

   10. Behavioral research: behavior modification,
   crisis management, human crowding, etc.

Figure 4.3   Round One Sample Page

Societal Problems

Delphi Round 2

The objective of this round is to prioritize the problems of
the refined problem inventory. An importance scale, identical to the
one which appears below, will be used to accomplish this task.

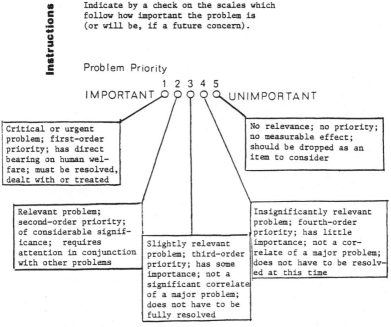

Instructions

Indicate by a check on the scales which
follow how important the problem is
(or will be, if a future concern).

Problem Priority

1 2 3 4 5
IMPORTANT ○ ○ ○ ○ ○ UNIMPORTANT

Critical or urgent
problem; first-order
priority; has direct
bearing on human wel-
fare; must be resolved,
dealt with or treated

No relevance; no priority;
no measurable effect;
should be dropped as an
item to consider

Relevant problem;
second-order priority;
of considerable signif-
icance; requires
attention in conjunction
with other problems

Slightly relevant
problem; third-order
priority; has some
importance; not a
significant correlate
of a major problem;
does not have to be
fully resolved

Insignificantly relevant
problem; fourth-order
priority; has little
importance; not a cor-
relate of a major problem;
does not have to be resolved at this time

As an additional index of importance, you may wish to speculate on
when a problem will reach its greatest intensity and then subtract
estimated reaction time to get a better notion of the problem's
urgency.

Figure 4.4   Round Two Instructions

A. WAR, PEACE, INTERNATIONAL COOPERATION

    1. Potential for mass destruction (regional and   1 2 3 4 5
global)   IMPORTANT O O O O O UNIMPORTANT

    2. War between nations over control of scarce   1 2 3 4 5
resources   O O O O O

    3. Internal conflicts leading to civil war and   1 2 3 4 5
threatening regional/global conflict   O O O O O

    4. Growth of armaments worldwide   1 2 3 4 5
                                                  O O O O O

    5. War related absorption of human and material   1 2 3 4 5
resources   O O O O O

    6. Nuclear weapons: control by governments;   1 2 3 4 5
potential access by small groups and individuals   O O O O O

    7. Inadequate basis for handling conflict between   1 2 3 4 5
nations   O O O O O

    8. Failure to develop suitable agencies to   1 2 3 4 5
maintain world law   O O O O O

    9. Obstacles to world government   1 2 3 4 5
                                                  O O O O O

    10. Inadequate expenditure of resources on the   1 2 3 4 5
search for peace   O O O O O

    11. Obstacles to cultural-political-economic
rapprochement: scientific/technological cooperation;   1 2 3 4 5
cultural exchange; automated language translation,   O O O O O
language standardization

    12. Diffusion of information/innovations on problems   1 2 3 4 5
in this category   O O O O O

B. POPULATION, FOOD, HEALTH

    1. Population

        a. Adapting to change in the population   1 2 3 4 5
        curve (exponential growth in many areas and   O O O O O
        decline in others)

        b. Contraception: obstacles to research,   1 2 3 4 5
        testing, and particular, use   O O O O O

        c. Abortion   1 2 3 4 5
                                              O O O O O

    2. Malnutrition and famine (agricultural production;   1 2 3 4 5
food storage-distribution; food surpluses)   O O O O O

Figure 4.5 Round Two Sample Page

Problem — Importance Scale Frequencies (Weighted Value)

Problem	5	4	3	2	1	x̄	n
A. WAR, PEACE, INTERNATIONAL COOPERATION							
1. Potential for mass destruction (regional and global)	23	5	1	1		4.67	30
2. War between nations over control of scarce resources	10	14	4	2		4.07	30
3. Internal conflicts leading to civil war and threatening regional/global conflict	4	16	8	2		3.73	30
4. Growth of armaments worldwide	16	9	4	1		4.33	30
5. War related absorption of human and material resources	8	10	9	3		3.77	30
6. Nuclear weapons: control by governments; potential access by small groups and individuals	21	6	3			4.60	30
7. Inadequate basis for handling conflict between nations	10	11	7	2		3.97	30
8. Failure to develop suitable agencies to maintain world law	5	14	4	6	1	3.53	30
9. Obstacles to world government	3	6	10	6	5	2.87	30
10. Inadequate expenditure of resources on the search for peace	7	6	11	5	1	3.43	30
11. Obstacles to cultural political-economic rapprochement: technical/technological cooperation; cultural exchange; automated language translation; language standardization	8		16	6		3.07	30
12. Diffusion of Information/innovations on problems in this category	5	10	10	3	2	3.43	30
B. POPULATION, FOOD, HEALTH							
1. Population							
a. Adapting to change in the population curve (exponential growth in many areas and decline in others)	7	16	5	2		3.93	30
b. Contraception: obstacles to research, testing, and particular, use	8	14	6	1	1	3.90	30
c. Abortion	1	6	15	2	5	2.86	29
2. Malnutrition and famine (agricultural production; food storage; distribution; food surpluses)	18	6	5		1	4.37	30
3. Conflict between goals of reducing population growth and increasing health care/nourishment	5	12	8	4	1	3.53	30
4. Health care systems							
a. Lack of equitable health care delivery for large segments of the population	6	17	6		1	3.90	30
b. Disease: prevention, cure, improved care, facilities (e.g., cancer, heart stroke, neurological, aging)	4	14	10	1	1	3.63	30
c. Birth defects: prevention, cure, improved care (physical/mental)	2	11	14	2	1	3.37	30
d. Psychiatry and mental health: prevention, cure, improved care, facilities	3	10	12	4	1	3.33	30
e. Emergency medical treatment	1	12	11	3	3	3.17	30
f. Need for more physicians (and other health care personnel) with improved distribution of services	3	14	9	2	1	3.55	29
g. Bug abuse (including alcoholism)	2	10	12	4	2	3.20	30
h. Artificial organs and transplants	1	5	13	9	2	2.60	30
i. Health care costs (including malpractice and insurance)	9	14	6		1	4.00	30
5. Genetic controls: cloning, creation of new life forms; selective human breeding	3	5	12	8	2	2.97	30
6. Redistribution of life, especially in such issues as abortion, maintenance of life in terminally ill, organ transplants, and artificial creation of life	1	9	14	6		3.17	30
7. Diffusion of Information/innovation on problem in this category	5	11	10	2	2	3.50	30
C. ENVIRONMENT, NATURAL RESOURCES, ENERGY							
1. Pollution							
a. Air	14	10	5	1		4.23	30
b. Water	17	9	3	1		4.40	30
c. Solid waste	7	11	9	2	1	3.70	30
d. Noise		10	13	6	1	3.07	30
e. Thermal	2	11	10	4	2	3.24	29
f. Radioactive	12	10	6	1	1	4.03	30

Figure 4.6 Round Two Summary

Societal Problems

Delphi Round 3

ROUND 3, First Task

In the first two iterations of the Delphi, we have examined societal problems one at a time as if they were independent of each other. Current research on the world problematique, however, portrays the problems faced by society as being interdependent, interactive, and systemic in nature. In this last Delphi round, we will lean toward an interactive, relational approach.

A method that allows us to begin thinking in relational terms is cross-impact analysis. Your first task in this round will be to complete a cross-impact matrix. The next section discusses some objectives of cross-impact analysis.

Cross-Impact Analysis: A Brief Description

Cross-impact analysis tries to predict the effect(s) that some specific event (or policy action) can have on the likelihood of another event occurring. It focuses on the relationship, if any, between any two individual events. It poses the question, "Does the occurrence of one event enhance, inhibit, or have no effect on the occurrence of another event in the future?" The answer may be expressed in qualitative or quantitative terms. Like the Delphi method, cross-impact relies on intuitive judgment combined with systematic analysis.

On the next page you will be asked to assess a series of impacts which occur when one problem rapidly accelerates and others remain relatively constant. From the cross-impact matrix we will be able to determine which problems most need to be controlled and the likelihood of actually controlling them. We will also be able to discover shifts in priority ranking which occur when problems are treated interdependently.

Figure 4.7   Round Three Instructions

A CROSS-IMPACT ANALYSIS OF PRIORITY SOCIETAL PROBLEMS

Instructions: The question being addressed in this activity is: "If, by 1980, the (insert problem ROW description) were to reach crisis proportions, what impact would it have on (insert problem COLUMN description) ?"

For example, "If, by 1980, the problem of securing suitable alternatives to fossil fuels were to reach crisis proportions, to what extent would the problem of air pollution increase, decrease, or not be affected?"

Using the scale which appears below the matrix, judge the degree of impact of each set of relationships in the matrix.

IF THIS PROBLEM REACHED CRISIS PROPORTIONS BY 1980 . . .	TO WHAT EXTENT WOULD THIS PROBLEM BE AFFECTED?								
	1	2	3	4	5	6	7	8	9
Potential for mass destruction (regional and global) 1	■								
Nuclear weapons control 2		■							
Water pollution 3			■						
Malnutrition and famine 4				■					
Alternatives to fossil fuels 5					■				
Growth of armaments worldwide 6						■			
Unemployment 7							■		
Inflation 8								■	
Air pollution 9									■

Column headers: 1 Potential for mass destruction, 2 Nuclear weapons control, 3 Water pollution, 4 Malnutrition and famine, 5 Alternatives to fossil fuels, 6 Growth of armaments worldwide, 7 Unemployment, 8 Inflation, 9 Air pollution

Maximum DECREASE in seriousness, magnitude, intensity						Maximum INCREASE in seriousness, magnitude, intensity
-3	-2	-1	0	+1	+2	+3

*The + sign indicates an increasing impact, the -sign a decreasing impact; and, 0 signifies no appreciable impact.

Figure 4.7 Continued

75

ROUND 3, Second Task: Resource Formulation

One of the goals of having you complete the cross-impact analysis was to secure collective respondent input on problem interdependence. In addition, this activity has likely provided you with insights on the complexities of societal problems and some ideas about the nature of resources that our discipline will need to contribute to have an impact on priority issues.

Before we ask you to suggest resources that have solution potential, let's briefly examine the question of what is meant by the term "resource." Usually, we refer to a resource as anything that is available for use, can be drawn upon, or can be advantageously brought to bear on a given situation in order to accomplish some end. Within this context, we may consider such assets as money, people, time, facilities, equipment, supplies, and energy as resources. Clearly, this list is not exhaustive; but a further delineation or even the establishment of restrictive parameters may hamper your creativity and innovation. Thus prescriptive criteria will not be presented.

There are, however, some task-related considerations which make the following minimal guidelines necessary.

Guidelines for Resource Formulation

1.   It is possible that our field has no resources to apply against one or more problems. If you believe this to be the case, say so without hesitancy.

2.   You may discover that a particular resource can be applied to more than one problem.

3.   As you match resources to problems, think in terms of two different sources of ideas: (a) <u>the conventional wisdom of the field</u>, e.g., our literature base, conversations with colleagues, recent journal articles, discussions at professional meetings, and the like; and, (b) ideas that are <u>new to you</u>. Here we are interested in ideas that you have never heard before.It is of no consequence that the idea is not "objectively" new-- it must only have perceived or subjective newness. Allow your imagination free rein.

4.   Attempt to show the relationship between the nominated resource and the problem: to which aspect of the problem does the resource apply, how does it apply?

Figure 4.7 Continued

Instructions: Match Communication resources with the problems about which you feel most knowledgeable. Place your candidate resource in the appropriate column(s) in accordance with guidelines on the previous page. You need not have both kinds of resources for each problem. In a sentence or two show how the resource relates to the problem. Indicate whether the resource is currently available (A) or is likely to be available in the future (F).

RESOURCES

PROBLEM	Source: conventional wisdom of the field	Source: new to you	How does resource relate?	A | F
Potential for mass destruction (regional and global)				
Nuclear weapons: control by governmental; potential access by mail groups and individuals				

Figure 4.8 Round Three Sample Page

77

5

Interpretive Structural Modeling

Carl M. Moore, John Gargan, Kenneth Parker

This chapter describes Interpretive Structural Modeling by providing an extended example of how the technique has been used, and by describing what should be done before and during the ISM session. The chapter also includes sections on viewing the ISM structure, a checklist of what is necessary to conduct an ISM, limitations, and resources.

Interpretive Structural Modeling (ISM) is a method of identifying and summarizing relationships among specific items that define an issue or problem. ISM provides a means by which a group can impose order on the complexity of the items. Frequently, ISM is used once a group has generated ideas through Nominal Group Technique or Ideawriting.

As the title suggests, Interpretive Structural Modeling permits a group to interpret, structure, and model its ideas. The method is *interpretive* in that the group's judgment decides whether and how items are related. It is *structural* in that, on the basis of the relationships, an overall structure is extracted from the complex set of items. And it is *modeling* in that the specific relationships and overall structure are portrayed in graphic form.

The ISM process begins with an *element set* that is composed of items relevant to an issue or problem (e.g., programs in a budget, members of an organization, factors that impede economic growth), and a subordinate *relation* that is expressed in a phrase that leads to a *paired comparison* between items (e.g., "should be cut before," "reports to," "will lead to"). The group is asked to compare two items (e.g., "In reducing the budget, Program A should be cut before Program B"). After discussion, the group's judgment is determined by a majority vote. The vote is recorded and usually stored in a computer. The group then proceeds to another comparison of two items. After all necessary comparisons have been made, the computer produces a model of the group's thinking, structured by combinations of the paired comparisons.

In a typical ISM session a computer is used to expedite the process. Reliance on the computer may attract or inhibit potential users. Use of the computer is attractive when people are impressed with its speed, efficiency, and neutrality. It is inhibiting when people incorrectly assume that the computer limits their discretion or control over decisions. During the ISM session, the computer simply

(1) stores the items to be compared,
(2) calls them up two at a time for comparison,
(3) stores the results of group decisions,
(4) infers certain comparisons based on previous decisions (e.g., if a group has voted that A is subordinate to B and B is subordinate to C, then the computer program infers that A is subordinate to C), and
(5) extracts an overall structure from the perceived relationships.

If there is a small number of items, a person could perform by hand the same operations. The computer saves time, effort, and money.

A Word of Caution

The utilization of ISM in a group context requires a sensitivity to both its science and its art. ISM is based upon relatively complex mathematical rules. It is essential that these rules not be ignored or violated by the user. It is not critical, however, that the user completely understand the mathematical bases of the method. In fact, undue attention to the mathematic assumptions by a group leader may detract from the effectiveness of the use of ISM, especially with decision-making bodies in applied settings. An equal (or even greater) influence on the quality of results with ISM is the skill of the group leader in facilitating the group process. Consequently, *do not overstress the mathematics of ISM, and do use the best available group process skills.*

AN EXAMPLE

A county board of commissioners faced difficulty in balancing its annual budget for a number of years, principally because costs rose faster than revenues. The board utilized the surpluses of previous years, reduced expenses and services, and increased revenues in order to eliminate projected budget deficits. Board members were dissatisfied with the means they had employed to make expenditure reductions and expressed the need for a more systematic, priority-oriented approach.

They decided to use an approach consisting of two steps. First, they completed a series of questionnaires to identify potential cutback units (programs or activities to be eliminated completely, or program elements). Second, they participated in an ISM session to arrange the cutback units in priority order, ranging from most expendable to least expendable.

The set of items for the ISM session was produced by the questionnaires. The paired comparisons were based upon the subordinate relation:

In reducing expenditures, should the board of commissioners
choose to cut
(item A)
before choosing to cut
(item B)

During the ISM session, a facilitator moderated the discussion of each paired comparison, encouraging the expression of opposing viewpoints. After everyone had an opportunity to comment, the facilitator called for a yes or no vote. A simple majority prevailed, with ties counted as "no" votes. Votes were stored in the computer. When all pairs of possible budget cuts had been considered, the computer provided the structure that resulted from the voting. Results were reproduced in a graphic and verbal format, like the one presented in Figure 5.1. Each item includes the number (reflecting the order in which it was considered), name, and dollar amount.

The ISM results showed the board's judgment on budget reductions. It presented a hierarchical format ranging from most expendable to least expendable. Items at the same level in the hierarchy were considered equally expendable.

The results were then studied and discussed by the board to determine if the structure produced by the paired comparisons made sense. If not, adjustments could have been made, within the limits of reasoned consideration. Chapter 6 provides an illustration of how one group systematically reviewed their product.

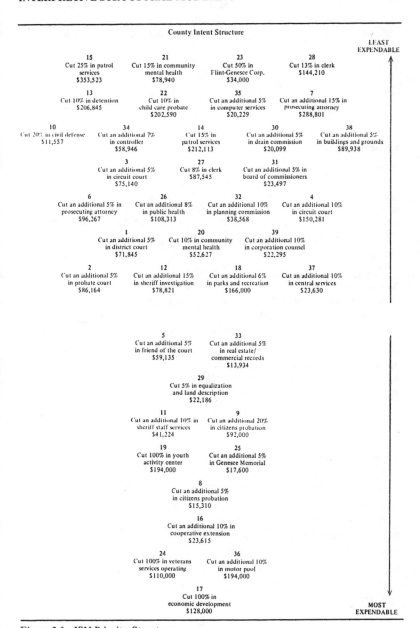

Figure 5.1   ISM Priority Structure

BEFORE THE ISM SESSION

There are a number of arrangements to be made before a group can engage in an ISM session. It is important to allow sufficient lead time for preparations.

Technical Arrangements

Item Selection

A particular application of ISM may require a large number of items. Moreover, when much is at stake in the results (e.g., with priority setting or budget cutting), discussion of the pairs of items can be extended and vigorous. For example, 25 items may require a full work day, and 35 items two full work days. Therefore, consideration must be given to how long a group is willing to commit to an ISM session. It may be necessary, due to the time available, to limit the number of items used in a session.

Items to be considered during the ISM session should be of major significance to the problem at hand and carefully worded so as to convey precise, clear information as briefly as possible. Near duplicate items should be eliminated. Less significant items should be set aside for consideration after the ISM session.

Chapter 7 provides an illustration of one way to manage a large number of elements.

Relationship Phrasing

The ISM product is based upon a series of group judgments regarding the relationship between two items. The relationship is expressed in a subordinate phrase (e.g., "is subordinate to," "reports to," "should be eliminated before," "is caused by," "helps to achieve"). The relationship phrase will be taken from at least one of six types of relations:

- impact
- influence
- definitive
- spatial

- temporal
- mathematical

Because the group is faced with the subordinate phrase each time a pair of items is compared, the wording of the phrase must be understandable to all participants.

On occasion, participants in an ISM session will ask that a subordinate relationship be worded to facilitate the comparison between items. For example, they might say, "Rather than deal with 'Is item A *less important than* item B?' [a subordinate relation], we should use 'Is item A *more important than* item B?' [a superior relation]." As the underlying logic of ISM assumes a subordinate relation, it is critical that the subordinate phrase be used throughout the session. The group facilitator should be prepared with numerous simple examples to illustrate the group's decision-making task. If members of the group become confused during the session about the subordinate relation, the facilitator should take time to remind them of the simple examples.

Chapter 8 provides an illustration of changing the relation so that the first element is superior (rather than subordinate) to the second.

Observation Charts

Forms should be available for recording the group decision and comments (on each paired comparison). Figure 5.2 is an example of the kind of form that can be used to record decisions and comments. Such a record facilitates analysis of the session, as well as the ability to continue or recreate the ISM process in the event of a computer disruption. In the event of a computer "crash" of some kind, the observation charts provide a way to reconstruct the work of the group.

Presentational Mode

A decision must be made as to how the pairs of items will be presented to the group for discussion and voting. Paired items should be presented both orally and visually. During the process, the group facilitator announces each pair and the pair can be displayed by means of

- A *display screen* (e.g., TV monitor, "advent" screen connected to the computer terminal). As the computer calls up item pairs, they are

CHOICES	VOTE	COMMENTS
e.g., 2 vs. 3	Y=yes N=no	Record reasons given for voting yes or no
vs.	Y N	
vs.	Y N	
vs.	Y N	

Figure 5.2 Observation Chart

displayed either in full text or with identifying numbers (e.g., item 2 versus item 8).

• A *display board* independent of the computer. It consists of a board or an easel or wall with blank spaces before and after the phrase expressing the subordinate relation. Items are recorded on cardboard placques so that they can be hung on hooks, taped to the board, or placed on a ledge. The following is an example of one display board.

DISPLAY BOARD (WITH ITEMS)
9. PRODUCTIVITY
has a lower priority than
6. FLEXIBILITY
when making decisions on
funding and direction

• An *overhead projector* or a *blackboard* could also be used in place of the screen or board.

Computer Equipment

Basic equipment is a terminal with a modem to permit access to computer facilities that have the ISM software. The terminal could be hard wired for direct (synchronous) access to the computer. Applications in the field are likely to use a modem. The modem can either use an acoustic coupler (which "cradles" the telephone handset) or connect directly into the telephone line. It is important to confirm the ready availability of a telephone and an open telephone line during the ISM session. If a display screen is to be used as the mode for presenting the paired comparisons, the screen and an appropriate cable to connect the terminal to the screen must be available.

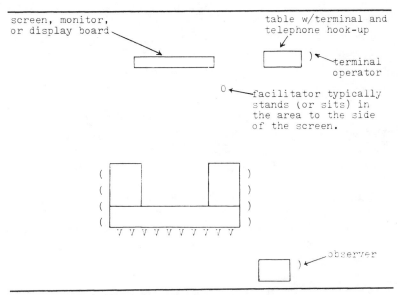

Figure 5.3   A Typical Room Arrangement

Computer Access

The ISM computer software is not available at all computer facilities. Arrangements for an ISM session include checking on availability of the program. It is also necessary to check about continued access to the computer. Although an ISM session involves relatively limited actual computer time, it does require an extended period of access to the computer. Probably the average amount of time for a session is three hours, and it is necessary to be connected to the computer for the duration of the session.

Room Arrangement

Figure 5.3 is a typical room arrangement for an ISM session. The key to arranging the room is to make it possible for participants to see one another and the display of the items being considered.

Personnel Arrangements

Although ISM can be managed by one person, it is desirable to have at least two persons: a *group facilitator* and a *terminal operator*. If a third person is available to be an *observer,* the output of the session will be improved as the group can then capture more information.

Group Facilitator: The person facilitating the group describes the process and the ground rules, presents the pairs of items to the group, leads the discussion so that all views are expressed, and brings the group to a vote.

Terminal Operator: The person operating the computer terminal must be familiar and experienced with the ISM program—including the software logic, program commands, and procedures. The operator is the link between the computer and the group and should be able to work effectively with both.

Observer: The person observing the session records votes and judgments and notes significant developments occurring during the process. Chapter 9 provides an illustration of the role that can be played by an observer.

DURING THE ISM SESSION

The Opening Statement

Briefly,

(1) Stress the importance of the task.
(2) Describe how the items were generated.
(3) State the goal of the session.
(4) Emphasize the potential usefulness of the product that will be generated.
(5) Summarize the steps of the process.
(6) Explain the role of the computer.
 The computer
 (a) holds the items,
 (b) calls the items up for paired comparisons,
 (c) records the results of group decisions,
 (d) infers certain comparisons based on previous decisions.
 (e) provides a structure that reflects the group's judgments.
 The computer does not
 (a) make decisions,
 (b) replace group decisions,
 (c) control the group or its decisions.
(7) Present the rules of the process.

- A majority vote decides.
- A tie vote counts as a "no" vote.

Conducting the ISM Process

The following is a procedure for considering each pair of items. This procedure is repeated for each pair until all comparisons have been made.

Step 1: Presentation

Facilitator	Terminal Operator	Observer
Controls which items are considered in which order and announces each pair of items as it is displayed on the screen or board. It is normally up to the facilitator to determine which new item the group will consider each time the computer is ready for one. It may be beneficial to start the process with a comparison that the group will decide upon fairly easily in order to foster a climate of cooperation.	Calls up the pairs of items for comparison when asked to do so.	Notes the item pair being considered.

Step 2: Discussion

Facilitator	Terminal Operator	Observer
Leads discussion of the item pair, making sure that all views are aired and that nonproductive conflict is contained.	Listens attentively in order to adapt the use of the computer to the needs and interests of the specific group.	Records comments on why one item is preferred over the other. It may be suitable for the observer to make observations about the group's process and progress.

Step 3: Voting

Facilitator	*Terminal Operator*	*Observer*
Brings the group to a majority rule decision on the comparison.	Types the decision into the computer and calls up the next pair of items.	Records the vote.

VIEWING THE ISM STRUCTURE

Shortly after the vote on the final pair of items, the computer produces the ISM structure so that it can be displayed for the participants. Figure 5.1 is an example of an ISM structure. The group should be reminded that the structure is based on its judgments about paired comparisons. Consequently, it may not reflect the group's best judgment when the relationships among all the items are viewed as a whole. The structure is, after all, the computer's version of the group's judgments. Modifications may be made in the structure and, if the participants are so inclined, they should be encouraged to make changes carefully, keeping in mind the discussion that gave rise to the structuring.

CHECKLIST

The following checklist can be used to determine whether or not you have remembered everything necessary in order to conduct an ISM.

Presession Arrangements

Technical:
____Terminal
____Modem
____Display screen, display
       board, or some other way to
       array the choices
____Computer time
____Item selection
____Relationship phrasing
____Observation charts
____Room arrangement

Personnel:
____Facilitator
____Terminal operator
____Observer

Summary of Process

Opening Statement:
____Importance of task
____Generation of items
____Goal of session
____Usefulness of product
____Steps of process
____Rules

Steps:
____Present pair of items
____Discuss pair of items
____Vote on pair of items

Review Session (if held)
____Examine structure
____Discuss structure
____Adjust structure

LIMITATIONS

There are a number of potential technological limitations on the use of Interpretive Structural Modeling. The most critical is that *you cannot conduct an ISM without access to a computer with ISM software.* At this time there are no microcomputers that can run the ISM software, so the software must be available on a mainframe computer. It is desirable to have access to a back-up system in case your primary choice is not available or breaks down.

Certain equipment must also be available. Minimally, you need to have a computer terminal, a modem (if the terminal is not hard wired), and a way to array the paired comparisons for the participating group.

A suitable meeting room is required. In addition to sufficient space and comfortable seating (the sessions can last a long time), the room needs electrical outlets (for the terminal and screen, if used) and a telephone or a modular phone outlet.

ISM can be fatiguing for the participants. Although the assumptions built into the software enable a group to deal with fewer choices than if they consider every possible pair, many decisions still have to be made. Moreover, participants are likely to complain because they have to consider some pairs both ways (i.e., both as "A is less important than B" and as "B is less important than A") and because it seems like they are "picking" on some items because they consider them in relation to many of the other items. This is why it is critical in the opening comments to stress the importance of the task.

In my judgment, most groups will be willing to consider 15 to 20 items. As you move beyond that number, the group must be prepared to expend an unusual amount of time and energy.

Special attention must be given to be certain that the elements are distinct and that the phrasing of the relation will elicit the desired product.

RESOURCES

Interpretive Structural Modeling was invented by John Warfield and introduced in 1974. The most complete description can be found in Warfield (1976). A recent overview is Warfield's chapter in Olsen (1982). Those who plan to use ISM should become acquainted with Warfield's work.

ISM software has been developed at the Battelle Memorial Institute (Columbus, Ohio) and the University of Dayton (Ohio). A software package can be obtained from Robert Waller, Dean, School of Business, University of Northern Iowa, Cedar Falls, Iowa.

6

Reviewing an ISM Product

This chapter describes how a group systematically reviewed the product of an ISM session.

After a group uses Interpretive Structural Modeling to produce a product, they may want to accept or review the product that has been produced. Examples of an ISM product would be a priority structure (Figure 5.1 in Chapter 5 is an example of a such a structure) or an intent structure that illustrates the relationship between a set of items. This chapter describes the creation and refinement of an intent structure.

One of the strengths of ISM is that it provides a group a way to think about the question it has raised. The actual ISM session, during which the group makes paired comparisons and then gets a display of the structure (created by the way they voted on the comparisons), may be the only time spent by the group in producing the product. The group may choose to accept the display as the final product because they do not have additional time to expend considering the elements or because they are satisfied with the product.

Some political situations place a premium on accepting a group product exactly as it is produced. If a limited amount of time is available for the group to deliberate or there is a conscious attempt to avoid what may be a rancorous and disruptive political climate, the group may agree at the outset that the structure that is produced will constitute the work of the group.

However, the display produced during an ISM session does not necessarily represent the final product of a group. The group members may want to review and perhaps modify the display because they are not satisfied with it or because they believe a review is in order. They may be hesitant about simply accepting one structure as the sum of all of their separate decisions.

A group might review its own ISM display, have one member (or a few members) of the group review and edit the display, or ask a process observer to view the deliberations and provide a description of the display (see Chapter 10).

ISM is likely to be utilized initially because the group wants a systematic way to consider a set of elements. That goal—of utilizing a systematic process—can be undermined if the group uses a review process that is not systematic. For example, the integrity of what was produced during an ISM session would be substantially undermined if after the display was arrayed by the facilitator he or she said something like, "How would the group like to modify this structure," and agreed to whatever modifications were offered by members of the group. The remainder of this chapter describes *how one group systematically reviewed an ISM product they produced.*

USING ISM IN STRATEGIC PLANNING

A county secured a grant from the federal Department of Housing and Urban Development in order to plan how the public and private sectors could work together to provide better planning for the county. Active participation by a group of citizens, the county executive staff, and the county commissioners resulted in long-range goals, objectives, and strategies in three major areas of county government.

Various group process techniques were utilized in order to enable the diverse group to productively contribute to the project. For example, 45 community leaders participitated in a nominal group conference in which they collectively identified 153 issues, problems, and opportunities that the county should address to make it "a better place to live in the 1980s." A follow-up questionnaire was used to determine the priority of the items and whether the county had a direct, indirect, or no role in addressing each issue. A group of public officials and subject-matter experts participated in a process to determine the relationship among the issues that the respondents ranked high in importance. This step—to determine the relationship among the high-priority issues—is the focus of this chapter.

The relation used in the ISM was "help achieve." In making the paired comparisons, therefore, the group voted on questions like the following:

In improving public services in the county, will...
18. EXPANSION AND SUPPORT OF PREVENTIVE HEALTH CARE PROGRAMS
Help achieve...
14. PROVISIONS OF ADEQUATE HEALTH SERVICES FOR THE ELDERLY?

Figure 6.1 is the structure that was produced by the group. Note that you read from right to left, so that item 3 helps to achieve items 9 and 19, item 9 helps to achieve items 7, 8, and 10, and so forth.

A decision was made to review the structure, and the group met again about a month later for that purpose. The following procedures were followed so the review would be systematic. The reader will recognize the essential technique as a variation of Ideawriting (see Chapter 3).

(1) The initial structure (Figure 6.1) was presented and discussed. Copies of the structure were distributed to the group and a large version of it on newsprint (approximately 6 feet by 14 feet) was taped to the wall.

(2) The 15 participants were divided into smaller groups of 3 or 4 persons. Each group was situated around a small table, approximately the size of a card table.

(3) Each of the small groups was given three different sets of ISM response sheets. Figure 6.2 is an example of one sheet. In designing the sheet, the assumption was made that it would be desirable to examine the initial structure (Figure 6.1) by focusing on the items that were related. Figure 6.2 is just one of many sheets that were prepared for the session, and it focuses on which items are related to item 13.

(4) The members of the small groups independently completed the ISM response sheets. This was very much like the "initial response" step in Ideawriting.

(5) The small groups discussed similarities and differences in how they completed the ISM response sheets. For example, after the members in the group considering the sheet in Figure 6.2 completed their individual, independent reactions, the group discussed the similarities and differences on their sheets. The purpose of this step was to stimulate their thinking about the relationship between the items and, if possible, to come to a group view of the items.

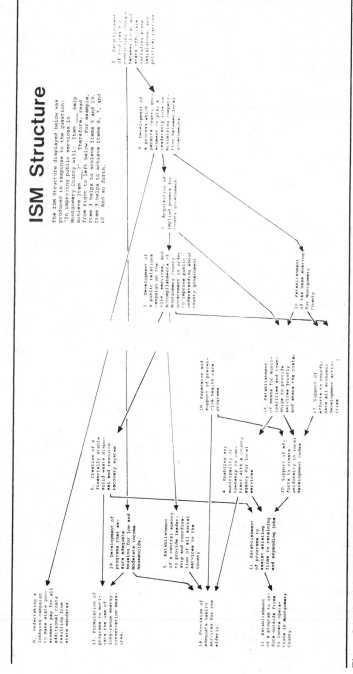

ISM Structure

The ISM Structure displayed below was produced in response to the question: "In improving public services in Montgomery County will: Item ___ help achieve Item ___". Therefore, read from right to left below. For example, Item 3 helps to achieve Items 9 and 19. Item 9 helps to achieve Items 8, 7, and 10. And so forth.

Figure 6.1 Original ISM Structure

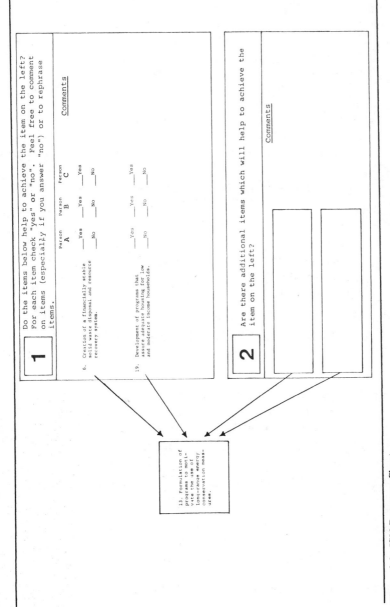

1 Do the items below help to achieve the item on the left? For each item check "yes" or "no". Feel free to comment on items (especially if you answer "no") or to rephrase items.

	Person A	Person B	Person C	Comments
6. Creation of a financially stable solid waste disposal and resource recovery system.	___ Yes ___ No	___ Yes ___ No	___ Yes ___ No	
19. Development of programs that assure adequate housing for low and moderate income households.	___ Yes ___ No	___ Yes ___ No	___ Yes ___ No	

2 Are there additional items which will help to achieve the item on the left?

Comments

13. Formulation of programs to motivate the use of long-range energy conservation measures.

Figure 6.2 ISM Response Sheet

95

(6) Each of the small groups reported to the full group.

(7) The full group reacted to the reports of the small groups. The group discussed whether the items in the initial structure (Figure 6.1) were *phrased correctly,* were *related* (e.g., whether an arrow really should go from 6 to 13), and whether or not there might be items that should be *added* to the structure.

This discussion resulted in changes to the initial structure (Figure 6.1). Figure 6.3 reflects the modifications that were made as a result of reviewing the initial structure.

A comparison of Figures 6.3 and 6.1 reveals that a variety of changes were made in the initial structure.

There were changes in the phrasing of five of the items. For example, item 7 in the initial structure was

7. ACQUISITION OF IMPLIED POWERS FOR COUNTY GOVERNMENT.

It became

7. ACQUISITION OF IMPLIED POWERS FOR COUNTY GOVERNMENT TO INCREASE SCOPE OF COUNTY ACTIVITIES AND TO FACILITATE JOINT COUNTY-MUNICIPALITY-TOWNSHIP PROGRAMS.

Item 14 in the initial structure was

14. PROVISION OF ADEQUATE HEALTH SERVICES FOR THE ELDERLY.

It became

14. ASSIST IN THE PROVISION OF ADEQUATE HEALTH SERVICES FOR LOW AND MODERATE INCOME FAMILIES AND INDIVIDUALS.

Two items (10 and 13) were placed differently in the structure.

There were changes in how items were related. New relations were added. In the revised structure,

- item 3 will help to achieve items 8 and 10,
- item 9 will help to achieve item 16,
- item 7 will help to achieve item 13, and
- item 17 will help to achieve items 6, 11, and 12.

Previous relations were deleted. In the revised structure,

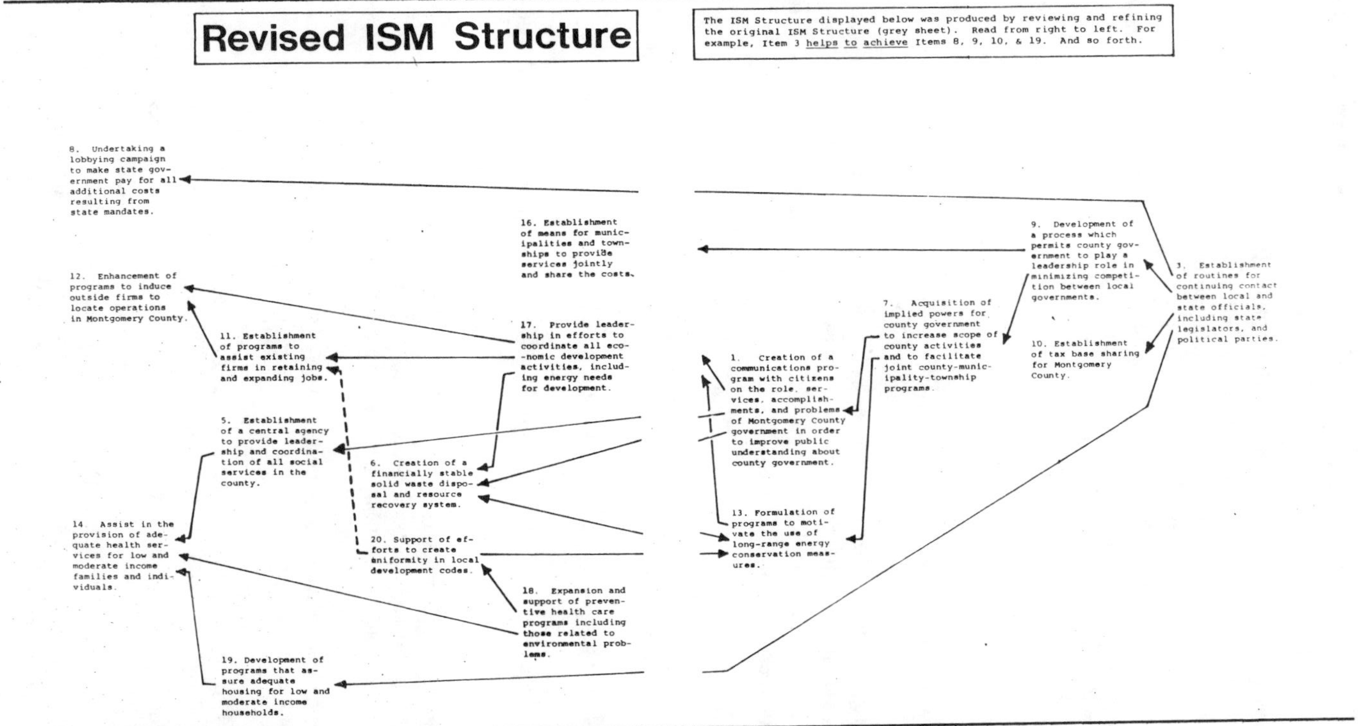

Revised ISM Structure

The ISM Structure displayed below was produced by reviewing and refining the original ISM Structure (grey sheet). Read from right to left. For example, Item 3 helps to achieve items 8, 9, 10, & 19. And so forth.

Figure 6.3 Revised ISM Structure

- item 9 will not help to achieve items 8 or 10,
- item 7 will not help to achieve item 16,
- item 10 will not help to achieve items 16 or 17,
- item 16 will not help to achieve items 4 or 20,
- item 17 will not help to achieve item 20,
- item 6 will not help to achieve item 11, and
- item 19 will not help to achieve item 13.

Two items (11 and 20) were related by dotted, rather than by solid, lines, suggesting that they were indirectly—rather than directly—related. The arrow between 6 and 13 goes in both directions. The arrow between 20 and 13 only goes to the right.

There was one deletion, item 4.

It is apparent that the changes in how items were related are at least in part due to the changes in the phrasing and placement of items.

The members of the group agreed that the revised structure was an improvement upon the initial structure.

SUMMARY

This chapter describes how one group systematically reviewed an ISM product that they produced. It was assumed that it would not be adequate for the group to simply begin talking about the initial structure they produced. Instead,

- the initial structure was presented and discussed.
- the participants were divided into small groups.
- the small groups, using ISM response sheets, reviewed related components of the initial structure,
- the small groups reported to the full group, and
- the full group reacted to the reports of the small groups.

The result was that substantial and seemingly beneficial changes were made in the initial structure. The revised structure provided guidance for the remainder of the strategic planning process. Participants working on different components of the planning process could use the revised structure to understand the interrelationships between various aspects of the plan. Once produced, the strategic plan was used by the county to provide policy guidelines for decisions that had to be made by various departments as well as the Board of County Commissioners.

The tentative lessons about group process suggested by this one application are that it is desirable for a review of an ISM product to be focused, that Ideawriting is a technique that can be used for this purpose, and that a systematic review of an ISM product is likely to produce beneficial changes in an initial structure.

7

Coping with a Large Number of Elements in an ISM

This chapter describes how to cope with a large number of elements in an ISM session.

It takes a substantial amount of time for a group to consider a large number of elements during an ISM session. If a group is properly prepared and committed to producing a useful product, they are normally willing to expend the time. But if they are not adequately prepared, are reluctant participants, or do not have much time, they may react negatively to the amount of time it takes and to the necessary repetition of items.

This chapter describes two examples in which I tried an innovation to enable a group to structure a large number of items by considering a small subset of items. The first example concerns a budget reduction process with a county government. The second example, also involving a county government, describes a group's attempt to prioritize a large number of potential work statements. In addition to illustrating how a group might manage the complexity of a large number of elements, both examples demonstrate how techniques are linked together in order to achieve a group-defined goal.

A BUDGET REDUCTION PROCESS[1]

A county government had an anticipated shortfall between the requested budget and anticipated revenues of $3.6 million, approximately 7% of the total budget. The commissioners were not looking forward to making tough decisions about budget reductions because they had done that the previous year and the experience was frustrating. They had avoided making some decisions the previous year by "drawing down" on (using) reserve monies. Reserve monies were no longer available. The controller thought the board would benefit by participating in focused deliberations. The commissioners had used a focused process a few years earlier and were pleased with the outcome.

After the decision was made to initiate a process, the following steps were followed:

(1) *Budget information was requested* from the controller's office (by the consultants responsible for conducting the process). The *budget information was reviewed* and *additional information was requested.*

(2) *A questionnaire was prepared* that listed each of the components that could be considered for reduction, provided essential information about each component, and asked the commissioners to designate the most desired level of funding (by an X) and the minimum acceptable level of funding (by a Z) for each component, Figure 7.1 is a sample of three of the items in the questionnaire. The general budget category is "Equalization and Land Description," and the first specific budget component (three components are included in Figure 7.1) is "Record Development—Master Tax Files." The number one (1) within the parentheses indicates that it is category one, which designates a discretionary service. Also included is the actual budget utilized in 1982 ($179,916) and the proposed budget for 1983 ($193,507). The scale reflects the percentages and actual dollar amounts that would be reflected at each percentage level. The commissioners/respondents were asked to mark an X at the spot on the scale they thought was the most desirable level of funding and a Z at the spot they thought was the minimum acceptable level of funding. The scale ranges from 0% to 120%, because it was not possible to indicate that a program should get less than zero dollars but it was possible to designate that a program should get more than 100% of what they requested. If, for example, the most desirable level of funding was 90% of the amount requested, that would be $174,156.

(3) The *questionnaires were distributed and explained to the board.*

(4) *Budget hearings were conducted* the following week in order to give the commissioners an opportunity to request whatever information they required in order to complete the questionnaires.

(5) The *questionnaires were independently completed and returned.*

(6) The *questionnaires were analyzed.* Two reports were prepared

MANAGEMENT AND PLANNING

Equalization and Land Description

1. Record Development - Master Tax Files (1, 1982: $179,916; 1983: $193,507)

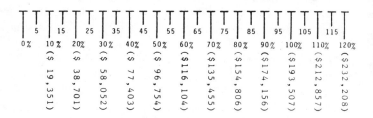

2. Valuation Analysis - Equalization (1, 1982: $379,686; 1983: $384,704)

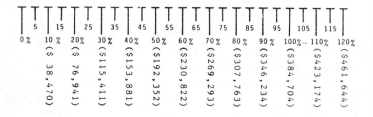

Revenue Management

3. Treasurer Accomodation Tax (1, 1982: $696,427; 1983: $709,935) --$3,600 has been subtracted from 1983 request

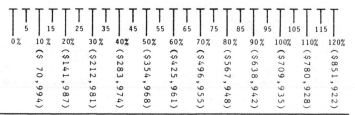

Figure 7.1 Sample of Questionnaire

that (1) arrayed the board's collective responses for each budget component (Figure 7.2 is a sample of the first report) and (2) described the implications of their decisions for the budget. Figure 7.2 indicates that on item "14. Real Estate Records," the largest group of respondents (6) indicated that the most desirable level of funding was 95%. Two people marked 90% and one marked 75%.

(7) *Interpretive Structural Modeling was utilized to determine the priority for 23 budget components.* A meeting was held with the board that reviewed the steps that had already been taken and had them participate in an ISM session.

The original intent was to conduct the ISM over approximately one-and-a-half days. The expectation was that between 30 and 40 items would be considered during the course of the ISM session. The reason for that number was that approximately that number of items were considered during the previous process three years earlier.

In order to keep the items as comparable as possible, only budget components greater than $300,000 were considered for potential cuts. This number was used as the demarcation because it provided about the right number of items. Once the arbitrary decision was made to use that number, the list of items above that amount was carefully examined in order to be certain that there would be a diversity of items in terms of the percentage size of the cuts, and that potential cuts were included from each of the sections of the budget. All of the components could not be considered in the ISM, so it was necessary to deliberate over a range of items that were both diverse and representative. The goal was to produce an ISM product that was representative of the whole budget.

Once the ISM was under way, it became apparent that the commissioners' interactions were not as energetic or as well informed as they were when the process had been used earlier with the previous board. Attendance during the course of the ISM session was sporadic, and many of the commissioners had not set aside sufficient time to work late that evening. It was decided that a concerted effort would be made to have the board consider items from each segment of the budget, but whatever the board finished the first day, that would provide the basis for their initial priority structure. In all, 23 items were considered by the commissioners.

(8) *The following morning, a questionnaire was prepared* that included the "first priority structure" (the 23 budget components) and asked the commissioners to "assign a number to each of the 60

14. Real Estate Records			15. Land-Use Transportation		
	Most desirable	Minimum acceptable		Most desirable	Minimum acceptable
100	XXXXX		100	XXX	
95	XXXXXX	ZZZZ	95	XXXXXX	ZZ
90	XX	ZZZZZ	90	XX	ZZZZZ
85		ZZ	85		Z
80			80	X	Z
75	X	Z	75		ZZ
70			70		
65			65		
60			60		
55			55		
50		Z	50		
45			45		
40			40		
35			35		
30			30		
25			25		
20			20		
15			15		
10			10		
5			5		
0			0	XX	Z

Figure 7.2 Sample of Board's Responses

[remaining] items to reflect your estimate of its priority" in light of the priority given to the 23 items constituting the first priority structure.

(9) *Questionnaires were distributed and explained to the board* at 11:00 a.m. that same day.

(10) The *questionnaires were independently completed and returned* within 30 minutes of their distribution.

(11) The *questionnaire responses were tabulated and a value was given to each budget component.*

(12) *All budget components were arrayed in one priority structure.*

(13) At 2:00 p.m. that day *the priority structure was presented to and discussed with the board.* It was explained that if a line were drawn at a certain point and if the board made the recommended cuts below that line, they would reach their deficit and would not have to make

any of the cuts in the budget components above the line. The spirit of the discussion following the presentation of the "priority structure" was that if commissioners wanted to preserve items below the line, they would have to develop rational and fair ways to trade off with items above the line.

It would not have been possible to conduct the ISM with all 83 potential budget reductions. Nevertheless, the intention was to conduct the ISM with more than the 23 that were eventually considered. Situational factors dictated the number that was considered.

It seems reasonable to conduct the ISM with fewer than the maximum number of items, so long as there are good reasons for the items that are considered. It is difficult for some groups to sustain their attention long enough to consider a large number of items. The first time ISM was used with the county board, it took them one-and-a-half days to consider 33 items. If fewer items are considered, it is more likely that such a budget reduction process can fit into busy schedules and the debate over items may be improved because the participants do not get fatigued.

Another difference between the first time the process was used with the board and this instance is that this time it was possible to produce a priority structure that included all of the budget components. Creating a partial framework (with 23 items) and then using a questionnaire to fit all of the remaining 60 items into the framework did allow the board to prioritize *all* of the potential budget cuts.

A PRIORITY-SETTING PROCESS

A county administrator directed all department heads to prepare work statements identifying major efforts. These were not to be statements of the obvious day-to-day activities but work efforts "over and above." For example, pumping 40 million gallons of water per day was considered routine. Combining city and county water supplies was considered over and above. Disposing of 1,000 tons of garbage a day—routine; installing electrostatic precipitators—over and above. Implementing an accrual accounting system, developing an energy conservation program, getting voter approval on a new concept for financing human services, and contracting for a new telephone system are a few additional examples of over and above.

After a new commissioner took office, it was decided that it was an appropriate time to educate and orient the new commissioner to the county's activities, as well as to prioritize, all at one time, the prospective work activities that were over and above, beyond the routine functioning of the county government. Interpretive Structural Modeling was selected as the essential process to determine the priority of county work activities, expressed as "work statements."

The Process

A series of steps was followed in order to identify the relative priority of the proposed work statements.

First, work statements were drafted by department heads. The statements were reviewed and some were rewritten (by the department head) to make certain they were clear, simple, and identified the specific outcome that would result if the work was undertaken by the county.

Second, in order to present the commission with work statements that were different from those generated by each of the departments (in the words of the county administrator, "to allow them to dream a little"), the county executive staff used NGT to identify additional potential work statements. They were asked, "If resources were not an issue and if you were a county commissioner, what is it you would have the county doing?" The 9 highest-rated activities were selected from the 30 the executive staff identified.

A questionnare was prepared and sent to the commissioners. The questionnaire included the department work statements and the items identified by the executive staff. If a justification was provided by the department head, it was included as a parenthetical statement immediately following the work statement. The commissioners were asked to judge whether each of the statements was clear and what was the priority (high, moderate, low, or no priority) of each of the statements. Space was provided for the commissioners to identify activities that were not included in the questionnaire but that they believed ought to be undertaken.

A training session was provided for one of the county staff and one of the commissioners to introduce them to ISM.

The highlight of the process was a day-long retreat to establish the priorities of the work statements. The county administrator explained the need for setting priorities. He commended the county's management personnel for their efforts in handling a large number of work programs and handling them well. The fact that this was being accomplished with a limited bureaucracy was cited as all the more reason why priority setting was necessary. He framed the exercise by stating, "With all there is to do, what would you have us do if we could only accomplish a dozen work programs this year?" Then the commissioners participated in an ISM session during which they structured the relationship between 19 of the work statements.

The limited time available (one day) did not allow the commissioners to consider all 115 work statements. Therefore, 19 of the 115 were selected according to the following criteria. At least one item was selected from each of the nine departments/categories. If there was a choice between general items with a policy implication and more specific items, a preference was given to the more general items. An effort was made to include those items where the responses to the questionnaire indicated that there were differences in perceived priority among the commissioners. Also, an effort was made to select items that reflected the range of the commissioners' priorities. All of the items ranged from 1.00 (high priority) to 3.00 (low priority), so approximately 40% of the items (7-8) were from category 1.00, another 40% from categories 1.66 through 2.33, and the remaining 20% (2-4) from categories 2.66 through 3.00.

Eighteen items were originally selected as the number for the ISM session because it was thought that was as large a number as the commissioners could consider in the time available. A nineteenth item was added because it was suggested by one of the commissioners in response to the questionnaire.

The commissioners compared each of the 19 work statements by means of paired comparisons. The same relationship was used for all comparisons. The following is an example:

IT IS A HIGHER PRIORITY TO

1. **Employ a licensed long-term care administrator as a permanent superintendent of the County Home**

THAN IT IS TO

2. **Perform a professional countywide human services needs assessment.**

A computer program was used to store the decisions and to provide direction to the group regarding which comparisons needed to be made. It took the commissioners approximately three-and-a-quarter hours (with an interruption for lunch) to complete the ISM. They made 98 decisions, rather than the 285 that would have been necessary if they had considered every possible comparison. They did not have to make every comparison because of the logic built into the computer software.

Within a few minutes of their last vote, the commissioners were presented with a second questionnaire that arrayed the priority structure for 19 work statements. They actually considered 18, rather than 19, work statements as one was dropped from consideration during the course of the deliberations.

They were then asked to put the remaining 96 work statements into priority order. They were instructed to use the priority structure they had created during the ISM as a "framework" and, in light of that framework, to assign a number to each of the items that reflected their estimate of its priority. It was explained that

> if a component has the same priority as the items at one of the levels (e.g., level 3), give it the number of that level (in this case that would be a 3).

> If a component has priority somewhere between two levels (e.g., between levels 3 and 4), give it the appropriate midpoint designation (in this case that would be a 3.5).

It took the three commissioners approximately 20 minutes to independently select an appropriate level for the remaining 96 work statements.

The commissioners' responses were tabulated. It was assumed that it would be misleading to use the arithmetic mean (the average) of the three scores, because if one commissioner varied significantly from the other two, the product would not represent the preference of the majority. Therefore, the medium—the midpoint—score was utilized. This decision protected the preference of the majority but did not make a substantial difference, as a test of the similarities between the commissioners' scores revealed that there was such a high correlation between the three commissioners, the similarity could not have occurred by chance.

The 96 remaining work statements were placed into the priority structure created by the original 18 work statements, and the board was presented with a 15-level priority structure that included all 114 work statements (see Figure 7.3).

Level 1: (HIGHEST PRIORITY)

CA4 CA5 HS1 OMB1 OMB2 OMB3 OMB6 OMB9 OMB11 PR6 PR24 PD3 PD7 SE5 SE21

Level 2:

CA2 AS4 OMB4 OMB7 OMB8 OMB12 OMB13 PR1 PR2 PD1 PD4 PD5 PD6 SE1 SE10 SE11 SE22 ES6 ES8 ES9

Level 2.5:

PR22

Level 3:

CA3 CA7 AS2 CED2 CED3 HS3 OMB5 OMB10 PR4 PR7 PR23 PD2 SE2 SE6 SE7 SE24 ES7

Level 3.5:

PR21

Level 4:

AS1 AS3 CED9 HS4 HS8 PR5 PR8 PR11 PR15 PR16 PR17 SE18 SE23 SE26 SE27 SE31 ES2 NEW ITEM

Level 4.5:

PR9

Level 5:

AS5 AS6 AS7 CED1 CED7 CED8 HS5 HS6 HS7 PR3 PR19 PR20 SE8 SE9 SE20 SE28

Level 6:

PR10 PR13 SE4 SE14 SE30 ES4 ES5

Level 7:

CA6 CED4 HS2 SE13 SE15 SE16 SE17 SE19

Level 8:

CED5 PR12 SE3 SE12 SE25

Level 9:

ES1

Level 10:

SE29 ES3

Level 11:

CED6

Level 12: (LOWEST PRIORITY)

PR 14

Figure 7.3   ISM-Related Priority Structure

While the commissioners' questionnaires were being tabulated, James Kunde, director of governance programs at the Kettering Foundation, discussed with them his reactions to their deliberations during the course of the ISM session. Chapter 9, "The Role of a Process Observer," is a written version of his remarks. One conclusion that Kunde shared with the commissioners at the retreat was that they dealt with more policy issues in one day than any other community had ever done.

The group adjourned after a brief discussion of how the priority structure might be utilized by the commission and the county executive staff.

RESULTS

This "experiment" demonstrated that a large number of elements could be managed by first considering a subset of the elements and then by placing the remaining elements into the structure that was created. Other results concern the operations of the county.

Was it useful to conduct the ISM session and to place all potential work statements into a priority structure? First of all, the exercise provided the commissioners with an opportunity to deliberate on the importance of selected county work activities away from the routine of day-to-day business. Moreover, as the executive staff was present, they clarified the meaning of certain activities and learned more about specific county operations.

Second, the commission produced a different structure of priorities than they had produced without the benefit of the paired comparisons and the interchange of facts and values. For example, two-thirds of the 18 work statements that constituted the ISM deliberations ended up at a different level in the ISM-related priority structure than they were after the priority rankings given them in the first questionnaire. Some were found to have a higher priority, and others were found to be of a lower priority, but the important point is that the priority was different after the commissioners had an opportunity to inform one another, ask questions of the county staff, and deliberate upon the relative priority of each of the items.

Approximately one week following the retreat, the executive staff reflected on the process and concluded that the process informed them regarding how the commissioners felt about issues and programs. They enjoyed the session, in part because it was not intimidating. At least one department was going to explore different ways of accomplishing their work statements in light of the feedback from the commissioners. They suggested that the ISM process could be used to get all elected officials to talk to one another, and that a similar approach should be considered for budget-cutting purposes.

The executive staff observed that, to avoid any confusion in using the process in the future, the work statements needed to focus on outcomes (what would be accomplished) rather than on processes (what the department would do).

An examination of the items by department revealed that the items within two departments were consistently given the highest priority: Office of Management and Budget and the Personnel Department. Any number of interpretations can be placed on that observation: The commissioners are concerned with efficiency and these are the two departments that can generate more efficient operations, these items are "doable," can be accomplished at this time, it is the right time to address these items, these are the departments in which there is the greatest need for reform, or, in the words of one of the members of the executive staff, "If you want an item to get a high score, neglect to do it; if you maintain the system, you will get a low score."

The county administrator reflected on the process:

> You might say that all of the work programs will be done eventually. So why rank them? Maybe your organization can afford enough staff to do everything, but most cannot. Besides, it was shown that items *believed* to be top priority were in fact not and that policy directions were sometimes totally misunderstood by staff. The entire exercise was enlightening to all. Even though we didn't end up identifying a dozen things to do "come heck or high water," we did develop a worthwhile, useful list of priorities referred to frequently by the Commission and staff.

In their year-end report, the county commissioners specifically identified the priority-setting exercise as one of the most important accomplishments of the year.

NOTE

1. The example used to illustrate ISM (Chapter 5) was also of a budget reduction process in a county government. It was the same county three years earlier. The following example illustrates an attempt to improve upon the first application. Two significant features of the second application were (1) having the county commissioners deliberate over a fewer number of elements during the ISM session, and (2) producing a priority structure of all of the potential budget reductions.

8

Using a Subordinate
Relation in an ISM

F. James Ross

This chapter describes a special problem with phrasing the relationship in an ISM session and offers suggestions for a preferred phrasing.

Chapter 5 explained that the ISM relation should always be expressed as a subordinate phrase, because that is one of the assumptions of ISM. A careful reader will note that the example of the county priority-setting exercise presented in Chapter 7 did not use a subordinate phrase. The relation was phrased:

IT IS A HIGHER PRIORITY TO
[itemA]
THAN IT IS TO
[item B]

That was done for two reasons: (1) to experiment with a different phrasing, because (2) groups tend to find the subordinate phrasing awkward. An alternative subordinate phrasing would be:

[item A]
IS A LOWER PRIORITY THAN
[item B]

The modification that was made was to reverse the order of items given by the computer, but still enter the answer given by the group. So if the choice that came up on the screen was 2 R 5 (in which 2 is the first item, R is the relationship—in the previous example that is "is a lower priority than," and 5 is the second item), the terminal operator announced it 5 R 2. If, after deliberating about that choice, the group voted yes, then yes would be entered into the computer. The assumption was that we would simply reverse the order when the computer provided the final structure.

The following is a portion of a letter to me from F. Ross Janes, who operated the terminal during the session, regarding why that should *not* have been done. He offers suggestions of what would be preferable ways to phrase the statement of the relationship. I include the letter because it is a lucid statement of a technically difficult problem.

F. Ross Janes
Department of Systems Science
The City University, London

On looking, a few days ago, at the matrix of the Commissioners' responses and the priority structure presented to them, I thought that it would be interesting to investigate the discrepancies between the two, which were puzzling me. ... I decided to do a rerun of the session to check the results, and then to see if I could reconstruct what the session might have produced had the questions been phrased in the form ARB [which was what the computer asked for] rather than BRA [which was how the choice was put to the commissioners].

RERUN OF SESSION WITH COMMISSIONERS (BRA)

I reran the ISM..., feeding in the decisions actually made by the Commissioners. This produced an identical digraph. ... [Figure 8.1] shows the matrix containing the Commissioners' responses to the questions BRA (the computer having actually asked for a response to ARB). Thus, for example, entry 4 R 7 (BRA) is 23N, meaning that it was the 23rd question asked to which the answer NO was given.

[Figure 8.2] simply shows the computer printout obtained from the ISM. [In Figure 8.3] the digraph... is drawn from the computer printout. This corresponds completely with *all* of the Commissioners' answers in the matrix. There are no discrepancies between the digraph and matrix, which is what one should always expect from an ISM session.

However, in simply deleting the relations in the digraph and presenting it as a priority structure, discrepancies arise. In this case there are 7 in all. I have circled them...on the matrix [Figure 8.1]. For example, to both 17 R 1 and 19 R 1, the Commissioners answered NO. In the "priority" structure shown [in Figure 8.3], elements 17 and 19 are at element 11 deleted during ISM session

BRA → A

B	1	2	3	4	5	6	7	8	9	10	12	13	14	15	16	17	18	19
1	\	2N		8Y	10N		22Y							66Y	73Y			
2	1Y	\	4N	6Y	11N	15N	21Y	27N			51Y	56Y		65Y	72Y	79N	85Y	92N
3		3Y	\		13Y	9Y		32Y	39N	47Y						81N		94N
4	7N	5N		\			23N							70Y	75Y			
5	(9N)			12Y	\		25Y											
6	14Y	17N	16N		18N	\					(52N)							
7	20N			24Y			\							68Y			86Y	
8	26Y	28Y	29N		30N	31Y		\	34N	41N	50Y	55Y	60N					
9	33Y	36Y			(37N)	38Y		(35N)	\	(48N)								
10	40Y	45Y			44N	46Y		42N	43N	\								
12	49Y	53N									\	58N						
13		57N									54Y	\						
14			62Y					61Y	63Y		59Y		\			83N		97N
15				69N			67N				64N			\	77N	90N		
16				74N							71N			76Y	\		88Y	
17	(78N)				80Y	82Y										\		98N
18	(84N)													89Y	87N		\	
19	(91N)				93Y	95Y									96N			\

Figure 8.1   Commissioner's Responses to the Questions BRA

level I (highest priority), whilst element 1 is at level VII. Similar, but less severe discrepancies occur with the Commissioners' responses to 5 R 1, 6 R 12, 9 R 5, 9 R 8, and 9 R 10, when comparing the matrix entries and "priority" structure. A true priority structure would be completely consistent with all the matrix entries and the digraph. In this case there is just not enough information in the matrix or digraph to give a true listing of priorities.

RECONSTRUCTION OF POSSIBLE
ALTERNATIVE SESSION (ARB)

Here, I attempted to reconstruct what the...session might have been like had the Commissioners been asked what the computer requested,

PRIORITY LEVEL	ITEMS				
LEVEL NO. 1	14				
	17				
	19				
LEVEL NO. 2	3	=	14,	3	
	9	=	14,	9	
LEVEL NO. 3	5	=	17,	19,	3,	5
	8	=	3,	8	
	10	=	3,	10	
LEVEL NO. 4	2	=	9,	8,	10,	2
	6	=	9,	8,	10,	6
LEVEL NO. 5	13	=	2,	13	
LEVEL NO. 6	12	=	13,	12	
LEVEL NO. 7	1	=	6,	12,	1
LEVEL NO. 8	7	=	5,	1,	7
LEVEL NO. 9	4	=	7,	4	
LEVEL NO. 10	16	=	4,	16	
LEVEL NO. 11	18	=	16,	18	
LEVEL NO. 12	15	=	18,	15	

Figure 8.2 ISM Computer Print-Out

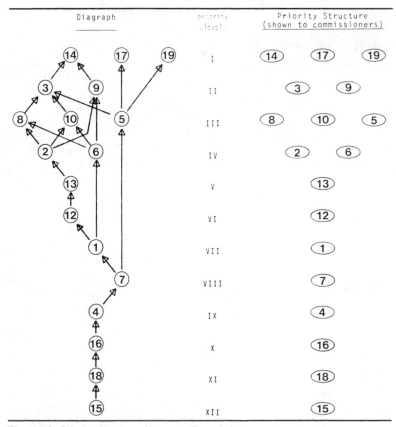

| Diagraph | priority level | Priority Structure (shown to commissioners) |

Figure 8.3 Priority Structure Shown to Commissioners

i.e., ARB. To do this, I ran an ISM responding to the ARB questions using the answers supplied by the Commissioners in [Figure 8.1]. In fact, the program followed a similar pattern of questions, as is shown in the matrix [in Figure 8.4]. However, it asks some questions not originally put to the Commissioners (indicated with a ... dot o). Luckily, I was able to infer the answers which would have been given directly from the digraph in [Figure 8.3]. Thus the questions 1 R 3, 3 R 1, 3 R 14, 5 R 15, 7 R 16, were not put to the Commissioners but are explicitly shown in the digraph [in Figure 8.3]. However, when I came to elements 17 and 19, the program asked for answers to questions which were not originally put and which could not be inferred (9 R 17, 13 R 19).

[Figure 8.5] shows the computer printout obtained and [Figure 8.6] the digraph constructed from it. Again the digraph is consistent with

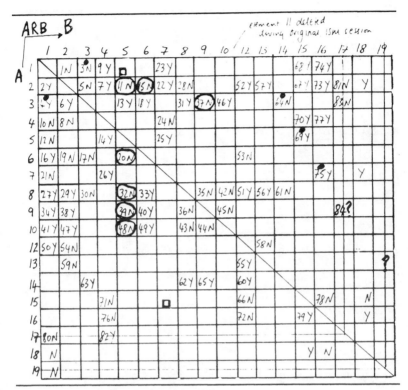

Figure 8.4 Responses to the Questions ARB

all the matix entries as it should always be. However, if one attempted to show a priority structure simply by deleting the relations, a false picture is produced. The discrepancies between this "priority" structure [Figure 8.6] and the matrix [Figure 8.4] are circled...on the matrix. Thus, the Commissioners explicitly said NO to 2 R 5, yet 2 is shown above 5, etc. It is thus not a true priority structure. Also, the so-called priority structures [in Figures 8.3 and 8.6] are different, although produced from the same information. . . .

It was clear that whilst the digraphs contained essentially the same information (excluding elements 17 and 19), the priorities shown are misleading. I thought that I'd better discuss the conclusions with John Warfield in case I had gone wrong somewhere. However, John agreed with what I'd found and has in fact written several papers dealing with this very problem. . . . One thing the papers show is that it would be possible to write a program which asked sufficient questions to generate all the information required to print out true priority structures

```
PRIORITY LEVEL  ITEMS

LEVEL NO.  1   15

LEVEL NO.  2   18  =  15,   18

LEVEL NO.  3   16  =  18,  16

LEVEL NO.  4    4  =  16,   4

LEVEL NO.  5    7  =   4,   7

LEVEL NO.  6    1  =   7,   1
                5  =   7,   5

LEVEL NO.  7    6  =   1,   6
               12  =   1,  12

LEVEL NO.  8   13  =  12,  13

LEVEL NO.  9    2  =  13,   2

LEVEL NO. 10    8  =   6,   2,   8
                9  =   6,   2,   9
               10  =   6,   2,  10

LEVEL NO. 11    3  =   5,   8,  10,   3

LEVEL NO. 12   14  =   9,   3,  14
```

Figure 8.5 Second ISM Computer Print-Out

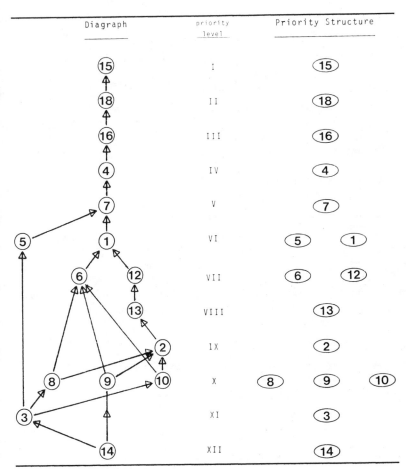

Diagraph	priority level	Priority Structure

Figure 8.6 Revised Priority Structure

directly. However, John does not think that this software has been written by anyone.

John confirmed that it is vital to ask either the question:

IT IS A HIGHER OR EQUAL PRIORITY TO
[itemA]
THAN TO
[item B]

or

IT IS A LOWER OR EQUAL PRIORITY TO
[item A]
THAN TO
[item B]

The phrase "or equal priority" in the question is all important as it will produce cycles and equate elements at the different levels. In the event of an element's position in the priority structure not being clear, this can be discussed and decided with the participants after the digraph has been produced. However, the inclusion of the "or equal priority" phrase will eliminate or at least substantially reduce the necessity for this to be done.

There are thus a number of important conclusions:

- • You cannot just read a priority structure from the sort of digraphs produced [in Figures 8.3 and 8.6].
- •• It is essential to include the phrase "or equal priority" if you want to develop a priority structure.
- ••• Inverting the questions put by the computer from ARB to BRA produces a different sequence of questions and different matrix. In this case the difference happened to be fairly small, but it would seem a risky game to play when doing an ISM in a professional capacity.

9

The Role of a Process Observer

James Kunde

This chapter describes the role of a process observer in an ISM session.

Chapter 5 explained that a person observing an ISM session can record votes and judgments, as well as note significant developments occurring during the process. James Kunde, director of governance programs, Kettering Foundation, played the role of a process observer in the county priority-setting project described in Chapter 7. Another person was responsible for recording the votes and the reasons given by the commissioners for their preferences, allowing Kunde to focus on other aspects of the deliberations.

His goal was to identify the criteria that the commissioners appeared to be using in order to determine why one potential project would have priority over another. The reason for trying to ascertain the criteria was the assumption that such information could be used by the commissioners to make future decisions. Earlier attempts to get groups to identify their decision-making criteria, apart from actually making the decisions, produced products that were suspect. It appeared to me and to Kunde that when political groups such as elected officials decide on criteria in the abstract, they produce what they think people expect of them, rather than what actually motivates their decision making. Hence, this was an attempt to identify criteria that were used by the commissioners as they made choices between potential work activities.

A REFLECTIVE ANALYSIS
OF DECISION CRITERIA AND GROUP VALUES

by James Kunde
Director of Governance Programs
Kettering Foundation

It is a generally accepted principle in decision-making theory that values guide decision criteria and criteria guide a rational decision process. In practice, however, elected official bodies seldom articulate values and form decision criteria that they use in decision-making. In fact, when decision-making criteria are explicitly formulated, they are often not consonant with the applied values of the group and are not adhered to in practice.

The use of the computer-assisted process of Interpretive Structural Modeling in elected body decision-making has provided a rational structure for public decision-making. The Commission utilized this process to rank 19 items which provided the structure for ultimately ranking 115 items in priority order for the 1983 budget year.

As the decision process proceeded, notes were taken as items were discussed and then voted on. As each decision was made, the primary decision criteria that "seemed" to be used was noted as well as any secondary criteria—especially where a controversial discussion pitted one criteria against another. The most frequently noted criteia were then compared against the structure of the 19 items originally ranked and examined for consistency. The results were then shared with the Commissioners at the end of the exercise to test whether the criteria seemed realistic to them when viewed as a whole.

As a result, of this process, the following decision criteria seemed to have been implicitly used:

1. *Timeliness and sequence.* Out of a number of important things to do, the most important criteria seems to be, "Is it the right time to tackle this job and/or is it the right next step in a sequence?"

2. *Efficiency.* Efficiency was not always the winning criteria, but it was the most important when the credibility of the Commission was in doubt or when there were too few items to show an image of efficiency in government. This suggests that an "efficient image" is very important.

3. *Doability.* This is a practicability test. "Can we really do this item, or will we end up looking silly for saying we'll do something we really can't accomplish?"

4. *Coordinator role.* The Commission was concerned that they were the highest local governmental level in the metropolitan area; therefore, they needed to demonstrate a coordinator role among lower level government to fulfill the image of being a successful institution.

5. *Consistency.* This was a frequently mentioned criteria that often lost out to timeliness or efficiency, but which held considerable importance when other criteria did not overwhelm it. "How does this fit with what we've done before and established as a pattern of action?"

6. *Protecting the public from overprofessionalization.* This criteria generally lost out to efficiency when the image of an effective county government was involved, but it repeatedly asserted itself in the human services area.

7. *Balance.* Whenever priority concerns began accumulating in one organizational division or weren't developing in another division, Commissioners became concerned that some areas of their operation might feel less valued than others. While this did not directly upset the other higher criteria, it frequently entered into the conversation as a comment aimed at an administrator whose program just lost out to another.

8. *Longer range impact.* This was clearly not a dominant criteria, but it did enter into the conversation fairly frequently. While it usually lost out to other criteria, it was important enough to bring up.

Values

If one looks at the above criteria in their apparent relative order of priority, it looks approximately as follows:

Timeliness

Sequence

Efficiency   Doability

Coordinator Role

Consistency

Protection from
Overprofessionalization

Balance

Long Range

This suggests that the primary values of the Commissioners relative to county government might be:

- Responsive—able to deliver timely, good services
- Holistic—broad in outlook and overview
- Humane and client-oriented
- Structurally balanced with capable people throughout the system

It might be interesting to see if future administrative reports to the Commission are better received if they address the above values and criteria. If so, the exercise suggests that it might truly be better to develop decision criteria *after* an exercise of rational decision making, as opposed to before.

10

Linking Techniques

This chapter explains that in order to assist groups, the four techniques are often linked together.

Seldom are the techniques described in the previous chapters used independently.

• Nominal Group Technique is typically used to generate items, and then some other technique or process is used to develop and/or select between the items. The example of the researcher who asked about the gero-communication problems of the aged (Sorensen, 1982; presented in Chapter 4) illustrates how NGT was used to generate a set of ideas that were then expanded upon, evaluated, and developed by using a Delphi. The other techniques might be used, but most often the process that uses the results of NGT is a traditional interacting meeting.

• Often Ideawriting builds upon the ideas generated by brain-storming or Nominal Group Technique. After Ideawriting has been used to sketch out a series of options, it is usually necessary to select a limited number of options. Chapter 3 included the example of a large meeting that used Ideawriting to generate a number of ideas and then selected some of those ideas and used them in an Impact Analysis matrix.

• Policy Delphis depend upon some other process to identify the initial choices for the first questionnaire. That might be a review of the literature or a technique such as brainstorming, NGT, or Idea-writing. The study of how the discipline of speech communication could help solve societal problems (Cooper, 1977: presented in Chapter 4) illustrated how a review of the available literature provided the initial options. The third example in Chapter 4 was an example of how the content of a meeting became the items for the first round of a Delphi. The product of a Delphi (or any mail questionnaire) typically requires analysis, as was the case in the budget reduction process described in Chapter 7. The monitoring team had to analyze and then communicate the results of the mail questionnaire to the repondents.

• Mail questionnaires are a form, and are therefore dependent for content on some other technique or process.

• Elements need to be generated by a technique or process in order to have an Interpretive Structural Modeling session. The priority-setting project (Chapter 7) used the work statements provided by the county departments. The budget reduction process (also Chapter 7) used the results obtained from the questionnaire (based on their budget).

Another reason the techniques are not likely to be used independently is that it is often necessary to perform a number of functions in order to conduct applied research with a group. It may not be sufficient only to generate ideas or to develop them or to select between them. More likely, two or even all three of the tasks need to be performed.

EXAMPLES

The following are additional examples of how the techniques have been linked together in order to help community, organizational, and individual groups.

Community

The *Citizen Attitudes Project* was undertaken to assist a citizen advisory group, which was appointed by the mayor to serve as a bridge between the citizenry and city officials to develop city plans, programs, and priorities. The two principal stages of the project involved NGT and Delphi.

Two NGT sessions were conducted with the citizen advisory group. One group responded to the question, "What are the major problems faced by the city?" and the other group responded to, "What specific actions should local government take in order to benefit the present and future residents of the city?" Thirty-two community problems and 36 courses of actions were identified.

The Delphi included three questionnaires. In questionnaire one, 34 suggestions of actions (a composite of the 68 problems and actions suggested in the NGT sessions) were mailed to 179 residents. The respondents were the members of the advisory group and others who reflected the diversity of the community. They were asked to rate the degree to which they agreed with each of the actions and to suggest additional actions that they believed should be undertaken.

Fifteen days following mailing of the first questionnaire, a second questionnaire was distributed to the residents who answered the first round. They were asked to rate the priority of 28 items on which there was a high level of agreement (from round one) and 32 new items, and to provide reasons whether or not to retain six items from round one that had elicited a wide diversity of reactions.

Three weeks later, a third questionnaire was distributed to the previous respondents. They were informed about their vote patterns on the second questionnaire and asked to clarify high-priority items that were ambiguous.

A similar pattern was followed in the Citizen Planning Program. The purpose of the project was to help set the agenda of citizen task forces by determining what citizens believed to be the major issues and problems facing the community. A secondary purpose was to train local citizens how to use the techniques so that they could help conduct the study and would be able to use the techniques after the study was completed.

NGT sessions were conducted with ten neighborhood associations, high school students, senior citizens, and others in order to elicit answers to the question, "What community issues or problems are of greatest concern to you and your neighbors?" Approximately 450 issues/problems were generated by the separate groups and then condensed into a list of 77 problems.

The list of 77 community problems was mailed to 270 residents (nominated by an advisory committee) and they were asked to rate the priority of each problem and to list other high-priority problems not on the list. The questionnaire was reproduced in the local newspaper and citizens were asked to fill it out and mail it in.

A second questionnaire, sent to those who responded to the first questionnaire, reported which items from the first questionnaire were given a high priority and asked the respondents to rate the priority of 73 new problems submitted in response to round one. They were also asked to select up to ten problems whose solutions would, in their judgment, best improve the quality of life in their community.

Organization

Chapter 6 is based on an example of how three different techniques were linked together in order to help an organization (a county government) develop a strategic plan. Nominal Group Technique was used at a community meeting in order to identify major issues, problems, and opportunities. A mail questionnaire was sent to those who attended the community meeting in order to determine the relative importance of the issues identified at the meeting. Interpretive Structural Modeling was used to structure the order in which 21 highly ranked issues should be addressed.

Group

The budget reduction process examples (Chapters 5 and 7) illustrate how a combination of questionnaires, group facilitation, and an ISM session was used in order to help a group of elected officials address a complex problem.

LESSONS

None of the techniques is an end in itself. They need to be utilized in concert with one another and with other processes (such as traditional interacting meetings). Linking the techniques seems to produce a "power" that is greater than when each of the techniques are implemented separately.

The reason for the powerful nature of linking techniques is that they contribute to group learning about the meaning of items. They allow people to look at the same thing from different perspectives. They also help to create group esprit, a commitment to the task and to one another. People want to get along, to work smoothly together, but they do not know how. These techniques capitalize on that motivation. If the techniques are used over time, they allow a group to get a gestalt of its issue.

Group techniques are important in solving real-life applied social research problems, because they allow people to combine judgment and knowledge. Intuition and analysis are not artificially separated.

All of the techniques are used to enhance judgment. There are no right answers, but there are better answers, and they are partly defined by whether people will use what they produce. People are more likely to use what they have a hand in creating. The techniques permit them to participate.

The techniques can be used in groups with varying levels of formal education. They can be used with groups that have no history or have a long history of having worked together.

Three of the techniques are easily taught, so that people can use them on their own. One reason they can be linked so effectively is that they are adaptable; the investigator is not locked into a rigid research design.

When the techniques are linked together, it is important to use them in such a way that results are produced quickly, with a minimum of machine/human interface. People learn when they quickly see what they did. Also, that serves to motivate them.

Attention to detail—in designing easily readable questionnaires, making certain people are comfortable during a meeting—pays great dividends. Attending to creature comforts will not assure a quality product, but lack of it ensures a poor result.

11

Criteria

This chapter provides criteria that can be used to guide someone in the use of the four techniques.

The following questions can guide your decision regarding which of the four techniques should be used in order to help a group be more productive.

Which function(s) do you need to perform? Do you want to generate, develop, or select ideas? The following chart suggests which functions are met best by each of the techniques.

	NGT	Ideawriting	Delphi	ISM
Generate ideas	+	/	/	
Develop ideas		+	+	
Select ideas				+

+ = Principal purpose.
/ = Secondary purpose.

Which of the problems that occur in interacting groups do you need to circumvent? Do you want to make certain that (1) the group produces more than a *few ideas,* (2) it is not *dominated* by one of the members, (3) there is *participation* by all of the members, (4) the group does not respond too strongly to the *status* of one of the members, or (5) the group is not unduly influenced by *political problems?* The following chart suggests which of the techniques would be most effective in addressing each of the problems.

	NGT	Ideawriting	Delphi	ISM
(1) Only a few ideas are produced	+	/	/	

(2)	The group is dominated by one of its members	/	/	+	
(3)	All group members do not participate	+	/		
(4)	Undue influence of status	/	/	+	
(5a)	Chairperson has too much authority	/	/	+	/
(5b)	Group rigidly follows rules of procedure	/	/	/	/

+ = Best technique to address the problem.
/ = The technique is helped in
   addressing the problem.

Which of the techniques enable you to secure the participation of a wide range of people? The previous chart suggests which of the techniques allow you to reduce the effect of status on the group. Additional concerns are which techniques (1) enable a substantial amount of *work* to be *accomplished in a brief time* period, (2) facilitate *contact with people who are separated* by distance, and (3) enable people to work effectively in *groups that do not have a history* of working together?

		NGT	Ideawriting	Delphi	ISM
(1a)	Consumes a small amount of time (so busy people can participate)	+	+ +		
(1b)	Produces substantial results	+	+	+	+
(2)	Involves people separated by distance			+	
(3)	Enables people to work effectively in stranger groups	+	+	+ +	

+ = The technique meets the
   criteria very well.

++ = Preferred choice among the
techniques that meet the criteria.

Which of the techniques best meet the assumptions of "second-generation" design methods? Which of the techniques (1) allows for *argumentation* of a variety of issues, (2) enables the *examination* of the relationship between issues, (3) can *clarify* ideas, (4) allows the client to *maintain control* over the process, (5) permits an *iterative* process, and (6) can be used even though there is *not a clear-cut image* of the solution. The following chart suggests which of the techniques best meets these assumptions.

	NGT	Ideawriting	Delphi	ISM
(1) Allow for argumentation of issues				+
(2) Enable examination of the relationship between issues				+
(3) Can clarify ideas	+	+	+	+
(4) Allow client to maintain control*				
(5) Permit an iterative process			+	
(6) Used without a clear-cut image of the solution	+	+	+	+

*A matter of how
the techniques are
implemented.

+ = Best technique to meet
the criteria.

Which of the techniques are the easiest to use? Which of the four requires (1) the *least amount of facilitation,* which requires (2) the *least support* (materials and technology), and which is (3) the *easiest to teach* to prospective users? The following chart rates each of the techniques in terms of ease of use.

	NGT	Ideawriting	Delphi	ISM
(1) Facilitation	4	2	5	5
(2a) Support: materials	2	2	4	2
(2b) Support: technology	1	1	1*	5
(3) Effort required to teach prospective users	3	2	4	5

1 = none
2 = little
3 = some
4 = substantial
5 = very substantial

*A real-time Delphi that
uses computers or terminals
will require substantial
technology.

All four of the techniques can be used in order to help groups to be more productive. The preceding charts should enable you to select from among the techniques in order to tailor their use to meet your particular needs.

12

Beyond Techniques

This chapter describes principles that are beyond techniques and that can be used to facilitate the work of groups whether or not the four techniques of choice are utilized.

The purpose of this book is to provide clear, useful descriptions of four techniques that groups can use to be more productive: to help them to generate, develop, and select ideas. The previous chapters have made a number of claims about the benefits of using the techniques, especially that using them will help circumvent problems that can occur in interacting groups and that the techniques will enable the participation of a wide range of people.

In order to achieve the book's purpose, it has been necessary to provide didactic descriptions that emphasize the stages of the techniques. Such an emphasis can be misleading, because it gives the false impression that each of the techniques is an end in itself.

The purposes of this chapter are to clear up potential misconceptions and to identify principles that group facilitators can utilize to assist groups. The goal is to identify principles that are beyond techniques, which are illustrated by but are independent of any particular technique.

The techniques presented in this book are not ends in themselves. Chapter 10 explained (and illustrated) that the techniques seldom are used independently: It is usually necessary to "link" them together to conduct applied research with a group. Previous examples illustrated that one of the techniques may be used to achieve a single purpose in a broader decision-making context. An additional example is when strategic planning groups used a variety of means (other than those presented in this book) to identify potential strategies, then used Ideawriting to generate and develop ideas for each strategy, and then met for a series of follow-up meetings to discuss the options that emerged.

A technique might be utilized to help groups do their work and, also, to realize secondary benefits. One important secondary benefit would be for the group to become more self-confident, to believe that they are capable of producing useful products. Groups occasionally flounder for a considerable period of time over their inability to accomplish assigned tasks. It is difficult for them to get "untracked." A successful idea-generating session using NGT (or one of the other techniques) might help them to perform one of their tasks and thereby give them self-confidence that they can work together successfully in order to achieve their goals. Once they have gained confidence in one another and in their ability to do work together, members are likely to be a more productive group in the future.

> Principle 1: *Groups will be more effective if the individual participants have an opportunity to think, and perhaps even write, before they are asked to contribute to the work of the group.*

Although groups are usually more effective than individuals in generating ideas, individuals are often more effective than groups when it comes to developing ideas. That is because research, analysis, and careful crafting of language—the skills most necessary when developing ideas—are performed better by individuals. Techniques like Ideawriting and Delphi are uniquely useful (compared with other group techniques) as ways to develop ideas because they draw upon the strengths of individual activity. Ideawriting allows the participants to write, and even to carry on written exchange of ideas, before they begin their oral conversation. Delphi, which is all writing, permits the participants to think before submitting their individual responses. While Nominal Group Technique is primarily useful as a way to generate ideas (rather than as a way to develop ideas), it reflects this principle when it asks the group members to silently generate ideas in writing before contributing them to the work of the group.

A group facilitator does not have to use any of the four techniques presented in this book in order to benefit from this knowledge about the differences between group and individual activity. Rather, he or she can act on the principle of allowing the members of a group to think, and perhaps even write, before asking them to contribute to the work of the group. So if you are about to ask a group to brainstorm ideas or even to discuss an idea, give them a few silent moments to think about the question or topic before beginning to talk.

> Principle 2: *Groups are likely to be more willing to select ideas if they are not forced into a win-lose, zero-sum position. Time and circumstances permitting, they prefer the opportunity to be reflective.*

Members of a group often resist selecting among ideas. Some resist because they are motivated by the desire to keep everything equal; they operate on the assumption that to give priority to one idea is to preclude other ideas. The traditional means used to select ideas—particularly voting—reinforce this concern. Voting encourages winning and losing; it permits a zero-sum outcome (in which my gain is your loss). Interpretive Structural Modeling (ISM) is perceived by group members as a useful way to select ideas because the paired decision making is a reasonable way to make choices and because the outcome is not absolute. Even though votes are taken, they are not single, final votes.

Groups often like to take "straw votes" to see where they stand, because such an action seems to be a less permanent decision. Instead of voting, it is possible to have groups rate items. Even ranking is often desirable to voting, because the group members are reflecting a range of choices. Sometimes it is necessary to vote and to abide by the outcome of the vote. Try and keep those times to a minimum.

Another principle that flows directly from experience with ISM is as follows:

> Principle 3: *Decision making in groups benefits from focus.*

Often groups are asked the wrong question if they are asked, "How important is choice A?" Choice A in relation to what? All other potential choices? ISM demonstrates that it is much more effective to present groups with two choices at a time, so the question becomes, "Is choice A better than or equal to choice B?" In Nominal Group Technique, one of the reasons for having a group revote is that they can eliminate the items that did not get any consideration in the first vote. That enables them to focus on a delimited group of choices. In a Delphi, the groups typically become increasingly more focused with each new round of questionnaires. Group facilitators can act upon this simple principle of "focus" by giving careful consideration to how choices are presented to groups. Even if an ISM is not used, it may be appropriate to ask the group to select between paired comparisons. One way to move a group toward closure is to get members' permission to remove from consideration items that do not have much importance.

Principle 4: *The effectiveness of a group can be enhanced if a group memory is utilized.*

Part of the effectiveness of Nominal Group Technique (and, to a lesser extent, Ideawriting) is because of the group memory. A group memory is when you record the work of the group on large sheets of paper and keep that work before the group at all times. The notion of keeping a group memory is useful even if neither NGT nor Idea-writing is being utilized.

Recently I had an occasion to mediate the differences between some "concerned citizens" and representatives of an Indian tribe. In order to encourage them to feel as if their concerns were being "heard," I recorded on newsprint each of the points they made and then taped the sheets of newsprint on the wall. This experience reinforced my belief that it is valuable to keep a group memory in almost any type of meeting. Compared to my experience in other, similar settings, both groups felt less need to keep repeating their positions (and, if they did, I could remind them that the position had been recorded) and did appear to pay more attention to the position of the other side. Groups are more likely to relax and have confidence in their leader/facilitator if they believe that their ideas have been captured. Moreover, group memories can be used to keep the group focused on the task(s) and even to deal with disruptive group members (Doyle, 1976).

Principle 5: *The effectiveness of a group can be enhanced if the group leader encourages the members of the group to build upon ("hitch-hike") each other's ideas.*

Most groups, unfortunately, do not realize their full decision-making potential. In fact, one of the principal reasons for the development and use of the four techniques presented in this book is to circumvent the problems that characterize most groups, to allow them to be more productive. Three of the techniques—NGT, Ideawriting, and Delphi—purposefully capitalize on the benefits to be gained from group members building upon the work of other group members. Participants

in NGT are encouraged to "hitchhike" on the ideas that are con-
tributed. One of the essential steps in Ideawriting is to react to and
expand upon the ideas expressed by others. The very nature and definition of the Delphi Technique is iteration; the group comes closer
together as the result of each group member becoming increasingly
more familiar with and building upon the work of the other group
members. But none of the three techniques has to be directly utilized
in order for the group to benefit from this principle. As a group
facilitator you can encourage them to build upon one another's ideas
and thereby realize one of the principal benefits of serving in a group,
rather than working as individuals.

Principle 6: *Groups are more likely to be satisfied with their work if they
have a sense of ownership of that work.*

Groups will take more satisfaction in their work and are more likely
to abide by their own decisions if they believe that they are responsible for the final product. Groups need to feel ownership for their
work. One of the things that can happen that diminishes a sense of
group ownership is that the group comes to believe that it is not responsible for the product that was produced. For example, if the person
facilitating the NGT session writes down what he or she thinks items
mean, rather than what was specifically said, the group can easily
disassociate themselves from the final list. If the items used to start
a Delphi do not ring true to the group (e.g., they sound like they come
out of a textbook rather than from their community), there is a chance
that the participants will not be prepared to sustain motivation and
the Delphi will falter due to a lack of participation. In addition, if
the contributions of an individual or a group of individuals is repeatedly
ignored, they will not want to claim the final product, no matter how
good it appears to be. The facilitator in an ISM should interact with
the group, but should never substitute his or her ideas for theirs. A
group facilitator must be careful to act as a process leader—rather than
as a substantive expert—or the group is not likely to claim ownership
of the product that is produced. Whether or not the techniques
described in this book are utilized, a group leader should keep in mind
and be sensitive to the need for the group to produce its own product.

Principle 7: *Satisfaction with group participation is enhanced if the group
has a sense of closure.*

In that the four techniques are well-defined processes, they all have beginnings, steps or stages, and ways to end. NGT produces a list of items and indicates the preferences of the group regarding the items. Ideawriting often has each of the groups report on the product that it produced. Delphi usually results in a forecast or a policy recommendation or at least a report. ISM produces a structure of ideas. Even if one of the techniques from this book is not utilized, it is beneficial to bring closure to the work of a group. The group leader should develop specific strategies that will give the group a sense that they have completed their work.

Principle 8: *No technique or process is any better than the people who participate.*

Chapter 2 explained that Nominal Group Technique is seductive, for both the participants and the group facilitator. It is easy for someone to come to believe that NGT, as well as the other techniques presented in this book, can accomplish more than is possible. The techniques obviously do not possess any wisdom in and of themselves. The products that are produced can be no better than the people who participate in the process. Planning for the use of any of the techniques must be qualified by the realization that one cannot accomplish more in a group than what the particular members of the group have to contribute.

SUMMARY

The four techniques described in this book are not ends in themselves. They are seldom used independently, they may be used in concert with other group processes, and they may even be used to realize secondary, indirect benefits.

There are certain principles a facilitator should learn about using groups as a result of studying these four techniques.

• Groups will be more effective if the individual participants have an opportunity to think, and perhaps even write, before they are asked to contribute to the work of the group.

• Groups are likely to be more willing to select ideas if they are not forced into a win-lose, zero-sum position. Time and circumstances permitting, most group members prefer the opportunity to be reflective.

• Decision making in groups benefits from focus.

• The effectiveness of a group can be enhanced if a group memory is utilized.

• The effectiveness of a group can be enhanced if the group leader encourages the members of the group to build upon ("hitchhike") one another's ideas.

• Group members are more likely to be satisfied with their work if they have a sense of ownership of that work. Maybe the converse is more important. The person facilitating the work of the group must be careful not to jeopardize the sense that the group—not the leader or facilitator—was responsible for producing the final product.

• Satisfaction with group participation is enhanced if the group has a sense of closure.

• No process of technique is any better than the people who participate in the process.

REFERENCES

Coke, J. G., & Moore, C. M. (1978). *Guide for leaders using Nominal Group Technique.* Columbus, OH: Academy for Contemporary Problems.

Coke, J. G., & Moore, C. M. (1980a). Group processes for making public expenditure reduction decisions. In H. J. Bryce (Ed.), *Managing fiscal retrenchment in cities.* Columbus, OH: Academy for Contemporary Problems.

Coke, J. G., & Moore, C. M. (1980b). *Toward a balanced budget: Making the tough decisions.* Washington, DC: National Association of Counties.

Coke, J. G., & Moore, C. M. (1981). Coping with a budgetary crisis: Helping a city council decide where expenditure cuts should be made. In S. W. Burks & J. F. Wolf (Eds.), *Building city council leadership skills: A casebook of models and methods.* Washington, DC: National League of Cities.

Cooper, D. R. (1977). *A Delphi analysis of priority societal problems and resources of the communication field.* Unpublished doctoral dissertation, Kent State University.

Delbecq, A. L., Van de Ven, A. H., & Gustafson, D. H. (1975). *Group techniques for program planning: A guide to Nominal Group and Delphi processes.* Glenview, IL: Scott-Foresman.

Dillman, D. A. (1978). *Mail and telephone surveys: The total design method.* New York: John Wiley.

Doyle, M., & Straus, D. (1976). *How to make meetings work.* New York: Jove.

Fowler, F. J., Jr. (1984). *Survey research methods.* Beverly Hills, CA: Sage.

Gargen, J. J., & Moore, C. M. (1984, November/December). Enhancing local government capacity in budget decision making: The use of group process techniques. *Public Administration Review.*

Helmer, O. (1981, May). Interview. *Omni*, pp. 81-90.

Lindblom, C. E., & Cohen, D. K. (1979). *Usable knowledge: Social science and social problem-solving.* New Haven, CT: Yale University Press.

Linstone, H. A., & Turoff, M. (Eds.). (1975). *The Delphi Method: Techniques and applications.* Reading, MA: Addison-Wesley.

Moore, C. M., & Coke, J. G. (1979). *Guide for leaders using Ideawriting.* Columbus, OH: Academy for Contemporary Problems.

Moore, C. M., & Coke, J. G. (1980). Engineering group interaction. In *Proceedings of the annual conference of the Society for General Systems Research.* Louisville, KY: Society for General Systems Research.

Moore, C. M., & Kunde, J. E. (1983, September-October). Setting priorities for Montgomery County. *County News*, pp. 6-10, 26.

Olsen, S. A. (Ed.). (1982). *Group planning and problem-solving methods in engineering management.* New York: John Wiley.

Sackman, H. (1975). *Delphi critique: Expert opinions, forecasting, and group process.* Lexington, MA: D. C. Heath.

Sorensen, K. A. (1982). *A Delphi analysis of the gero-communications needs of the aged in Marquette County, Michigan.* Unpublished doctoral dissertation, Kent State University.

Strauch, R. E. (1974). *A critical assessment of quantitative methodology as a policy analysis tool.* Santa Monica, CA: Rand.

Thissen, W.A.H., Sage, A. P., & Warfield, J. N. (1980). *A users' guide to public systems methodology.* Charlottesville, VA: School of Engineering and Applied Science.

Turoff, M. (1975). The policy Delphi. In H. A. Linstone & M. Turoff (Eds.), *The Delphi Method: Techniques and applications.* Reading, MA: Addison-Wesley.

Warfield, J. N. (1976). *Societal systems: Planning, policy, and complexity.* New York: John Wiley.

Warfield, J. N. (1982). *Consensus methodologies.* Charlottesville, VA: Center for Interactive Management.

Weiss, C. H. (Ed.). (1977). *Using social research in public policy making.* Lexington, MA: Lexington Books.

Williams, H. (1980). Some thoughts on pursuing goals in the three-county area. In C. M. Moore, H. Williams, & S. Shapiro (Eds.), *What issues, problems, and opportunities should be addressed in order to make the three-county region of Adair, Cherokee, and Sequoyah a better place to live in the 1980s?* Dayton, OH: Kettering Foundation.

ABOUT THE AUTHOR

Carl M. Moore is Professor in Speech Communication at Kent State University. A former Fellow of the Academy for Contemporary Problems and the National Training and Development Service, he is currently an Associate of the Kettering Foundation and is a Senior Associate in community problem solving with the Urban Center of the College of Urban Affairs at Cleveland State University.

Dr. Moore was responsible (along with James G. Coke) for the development of the Negotiated Investment Strategy (NIS) model, and evaluated the first applications of NIS in St. Paul, MN, Columbus, OH, Gary, IN, and for the state of Connecticut. On two occasions he mediated the state of Mississippi's allocation of their Social Service Bloc Grant monies. He has been responsible for negotiating faculty contracts at Kent State University, and for facilitating/mediating disputes involving the Cherokee Nation, Winnebago Indians, Connecticut Social Service Tri-Partite Commission, various public service agencies, foundations, and local and state governments.

Dr. Moore has served as a consultant for several federal, state, and city agencies, and has assisted community leadership programs in Baltimore, Chicago, Cleveland, and many other cities. He works with the Lilly Endowment on their program in community leadership, the board of the National Association of Community Leadership Organizations (NACLO), and has planned and presented programs at NACLO national conferences.

His publications include articles in *Nation's Cities Weekly, Journal of Intergroup Relations, Communication Strategies in the Practice of Lawyering,* and *Public Administration Review.*

NOTES